Politics *with* the People

Many citizens in the United States and abroad fear that democratic institutions have become weak, and continue to weaken. *Politics* with *the People* develops the principles and practice of "directly representative democracy" – a new way of connecting citizens and elected officials to improve representative government. Sitting members of Congress agreed to meet with groups of their constituents via online, deliberative town hall meetings to discuss some of the most important and controversial issues of the day. The results from these experiments reveal a model of how our democracy could work, where politicians consult with and inform citizens in substantive discussions, and where otherwise marginalized citizens participate and are empowered. Moving beyond our broken system of interest-group politics and partisan blood sport, directly representative reforms will help restore citizens' faith in the institutions of democratic self-government, precisely at a time when those institutions themselves feel dysfunctional and endangered.

Michael A. Neblo is Associate Professor of Political Science and (by courtesy) Philosophy and Public Policy, and Director of the Institute for Democratic Engagement and Accountability (IDEA) at The Ohio State University.

Kevin M. Esterling is Professor of Public Policy and Political Science at the University of California, Riverside.

David M. J. Lazer is Distinguished Professor of Political Science and Computer and Information Science, and Co-Director of the NULab for Texts, Maps, and Networks at Northeastern University and a Visiting Scholar at the Institute for Quantitative Social Science at Harvard University.

Cambridge Studies in Public Opinion and Political Psychology

Series Editors
Dennis Chong, *University of Southern California and Northwestern University*
James H. Kuklinksi, *University of Illinois, Urbana-Champaign*

Cambridge Studies in Public Opinion and Political Psychology publishes innovative research from a variety of theoretical and methodological perspectives on the mass public foundations of politics and society. Research in the series focuses on the origins and influence of mass opinion, the dynamics of information and deliberation, and the emotional, normative, and instrumental bases of political choice. In addition to examining psychological processes, the series explores the organization of groups, the association between individual and collective preferences, and the impact of institutions on beliefs and behavior.

Cambridge Studies in Public Opinion and Political Psychology is dedicated to furthering theoretical and empirical research on the relationship between the political system and the attitudes and actions of citizens.

Books in the series are listed on the page following the Index.

Politics *with* the People

Building *a* Directly Representative Democracy

MICHAEL A. NEBLO

The Ohio State University

KEVIN M. ESTERLING

University of California, Riverside

DAVID M.J. LAZER

Northeastern University/ Harvard University

CAMBRIDGE
UNIVERSITY PRESS

CAMBRIDGE
UNIVERSITY PRESS

University Printing House, Cambridge CB2 8BS, United Kingdom

One Liberty Plaza, 20th Floor, New York, NY 10006, USA

477 Williamstown Road, Port Melbourne, VIC 3207, Australia

314–321, 3rd Floor, Plot 3, Splendor Forum, Jasola District Centre, New Delhi – 110025, India

79 Anson Road, #06-04/06, Singapore 079906

Cambridge University Press is part of the University of Cambridge.

It furthers the University's mission by disseminating knowledge in the pursuit of education, learning, and research at the highest international levels of excellence.

www.cambridge.org
Information on this title: www.cambridge.org/9781107117266
DOI: 10.1017/9781316338179

© Michael A. Neblo, Kevin M. Esterling and David M. J. Lazer 2018

First published 2018

Printed in the United States of America by Sheridan Books, Inc.

A catalogue record for this publication is available from the British Library.

ISBN 978-1-107-11726-6 Hardback

MN: For Eileen, Anna, and Kate – the people I'm building
a life with.

KE: To my wonderful wife Emily, who is always there for me
when I need constructive, two-way communication, and to my
two kids, Zachary and Cadence, who excel in direct and deliberative engagement (sometimes with their parents).

DL: I dedicate this volume to the memories and legacies of my
grandmother, Lina Dinerstein, and of my mother, Estelle James,
both of whom died during work on this book. My grandmother,
born in Austria-Hungary, fled from Cossacks when she was a
child, was a refugee during World War I, and immigrated to New
York shortly after the war ended. My mother was an economist –
one of the first women to receive her PhD in economics from
MIT – and whose work on pension reform has benefited millions
of people around the world. It was in her house in Washington
that we conceived much of the early work on this project. They
had the power of imagination and force of will to create a better
world for the next generation.

Designs are brought to nothing where there is no counsel:
But in the multitude of counselors they succeed.

– Proverbs 15:22

Contents

Figures

Tables

Acknowledgments

This book is about people coming together in dialogue to build something new and worthwhile. We want to begin, then, by thanking those who entered into dialogue with us to build the book itself. Anything worthwhile in what we have written is due, in large part, to them.

The dialogue began with a phone call from Brad Fitch of the Congressional Management Foundation (CMF). Brad proposed joint research on how to help Congressional offices use new communications technology to serve their constituents better – that is, to improve the way that representative democracy works. In some ways, this whole project was CMF's idea. We have been extraordinarily fortunate to have them adopt us into their organizational family. We thank the entire CMF team, especially its three successive executive directors during this project: Rick Shapiro, Beverly Bell, and Brad Fitch. CMF's remarkable research staff – Kathy Goldschmidt, Nicole Folk Cooper, Collin Burden, and Tim Hysom – taught us more about Congress than any of our courses in graduate school. That we owe CMF a tremendous debt of gratitude goes without saying. What most people do not realize, however, is that the whole nation, really, owes a similar debt of gratitude for the daily, unheralded work CMF does to help Congress serve our country better.

Our collaboration with CMF led to a grant from the National Science Foundation's Digital Government Program.[1] We thank NSF, and our

[1] This material is based upon work supported by the National Science Foundation under Grant No. (IIS-0429452). Any opinions, findings, and conclusions or recommendations expressed in this material are those of the authors and do not necessarily reflect the views of the National Science Foundation.

program manager, the late Larry Brandt, for the confidence he had in a group of (then) young investigators. Larry was a visionary public servant who empowered a generation of scholars to think creatively about democracy, governance, and technology. The deliberative town hall with Senator Carl Levin was funded by a generous grant from the Ash Institute for Democratic Governance & Innovation at Harvard's Kennedy School of Government. We thank the Institute, and its director, Tony Saich, for their enthusiastic support.

We are extremely grateful to the thirteen members of Congress who were brave enough to serve as test pilots for our institutional innovations: Earl Blumenauer, Michael Capuano, James Clyburn, Mike Conaway, Anna Eshoo, Jack Kingston, Carl Levin, Zoe Lofgren, Don Manzullo, Jim Matheson, David Price, George Radanovich, and Dave Weldon. As a noted political advisor once said, "There is nothing more difficult to take in hand, more perilous to conduct, or more uncertain in its success, than to take the lead in the introduction of a new order of things." We appreciate the willingness of these thirteen public servants to take a chance with us to imagine a new order of constituent communication.

It is not customary for public opinion researchers to thank their sample of respondents. But the over 2,000 people who participated in our study were not merely "subjects" in our experiments. They are, and were acting as, our fellow citizens. Those who talked to their representatives took the time to engage in a form of real (if unusual) politics. They made their voices heard in the democratic process in a way that goes beyond voting, donating, or shouting. For this, we are deeply grateful.

Three colleagues stand out for special thanks because of their crucial contributions to this project. In addition to coauthoring the articles on which Chapters 3 and 7 are based, Anand Sokhey provided detailed and helpful feedback on the entire manuscript at a crucial juncture. Ryan Kennedy, also a coauthor on those papers, currently leads the team conducting our second wave of research on consultation with Congress. (Thus, any remaining questions you have upon finishing this book should be directed to Ryan.) William Minozzi was the lead author on a paper with results crucial to Chapters 5 and 6. In addition to his extensive and insightful comments on the manuscript, William devoted a session of his graduate course to discussing a draft. We thank both him and the participants in the seminar for their helpful feedback. William is also a key member of the second wave research team.

We have had much encouragement and feedback from colleagues and friends throughout the process of researching and writing this book.

Jenny Mansbridge, a constant inspiration as a scholar and colleague, advocated for and mentored us through the entire project, and provided very detailed and helpful comments on the manuscript. André Bächtiger, Jamie Druckman, Peter Levine, Stefan McCabe, Tanja Pritzlaff, Sarah Shugars, and Craig Volden all read the entire manuscript and offered timely and invaluable feedback. For conversations about various elements of the project we thank John Dedrick, Dan Esterling, Donald Esterling, Linda Esterling, Nick Felts, Jane Fountain, Jon Green, Don Hubin, Jon Kingzette, Rick Herrmann, Amy Lee, Sandra Levy-Achtemeier, Eric MacGilvray, Ben McKean, Eileen McMahon, Ines Mergel, Laura Moses, Tom Nelson, Alexander Schellong, Piers Turner, Inés Valdez, Charlotte Weber, Steve Zeller, and Curt Ziniel, as well as participants in seminars at the University of Bremen, Harvard University, the Kettering Foundation, Northeastern University, the University of Notre Dame, Ohio State University, and Villa Vigoni. Jon Green and Jon Kingzette provided remarkably fast and reliable assistance preparing the manuscript for final publication.

Special thanks to our editor at Cambridge University Press, Robert Dreesen. Robert's early encouragement helped us to see the value of synthesizing the disparate findings in journal articles into something bigger and more coherent. His continuing encouragement and support over the years have shaped every dimension of the book, all for the better.

Strange as it may sound, the three of us would like publicly to thank each other. Our growth as colleagues and friends through this project has been among the most rewarding experiences of our careers.

Acknowledgments to families are often a mix of gratitude and apology, and we can fully appreciate why. We want to express our profound thanks to Eileen McMahon, Emily Garabedian, and Lisa Bernt. This book reflects their thoughtful comments, their support when it took us away from home, and their patience as it (slowly) materialized. And for our children, we regret the times we have been absent (literally or figuratively), and hope for a world in which their voices will be heard.

Introduction

Directly Representative Democracy

Here, sir, the people govern; here they act by their immediate representatives.
—Alexander Hamilton, 1788[1]

Today, Hamilton's boast is more likely to elicit cynical laughter than reverential striving. Many will recognize his picture of democracy from their middle school civics textbooks. We are taught quotations like these as children in order to connect our first ideas about politics to the Founders' vision of representative government. Doing so can serve worthy purposes. Fostering such ideals early can inspire us to work toward realizing them as adults. Yet many citizens now believe that Hamilton's picture has been turned upside-down. Far from self-governing, they feel alienated by the trench warfare of partisan elites. Far from being empowered to act, they feel paralyzed by the complexity of modern governance. And far from having the ear of their "immediate" representatives, they feel remote from them, their voices drowned out by the clamor of interposed special interests.[2] The gap between our civics textbook pictures of representative democracy and our lived experience feels large and growing.

---

[1] Jonathan Elliot, *The Debates in the Several State Conventions on the Adoption of the Federal Constitution: As Recommended by the General Convention at Philadelphia in 1787* (Vol. 2, 1866), 348. Published under the Sanction of Congress, Accessed May 28, 2018. https://memory.loc.gov/cgi-bin/query/r?ammem/hlaw:@field(DOCID+@lit(ed0021)). These remarks were made at the New York convention on the adoption of the federal Constitution in Poughkeepsie, New York on June 27, 1788. Hamilton was referring to the House of Representatives.

[2] See, for example, a recent poll by AP-NORC, where 65 percent of Americans believe that political lobbyists have too much influence in DC, while 75 percent state that people like themselves have too little influence. "Views on Power and Influence in Washington,"

This gap is felt beyond the United States as well. Strained relationships between citizens and their representatives have led to accusations of "democratic deficits" against European Union technocrats. In the United Kingdom, citizens split with most experts and officials on the "Brexit" referendum. And more generally, resurgent nationalism across much of the globe is rejecting many mainstream parties.

In the United States, trust and approval of Congress remains near its all-time low (9 percent).[3] Populist challenges, driven by anxiety and alienation, are roiling both major parties, and fueling our own nationalist backlash. Even politicians themselves express frustration and dismay, notably in their retirement speeches.[4] Hamilton's picture of the people governing in a meaningful way seems quaint, perhaps even funny, if the stakes were not so deadly serious. Many citizens believe that interest-group capture and partisan bloodsport have disfigured beyond recognition any such portrait of authentically acting through our immediate representatives.[5]

Given this dissatisfaction, reformers have naturally begun contemplating changes that might help remediate the problems besetting representative

---

APNORC.org, Accessed May 28, 2018. www.apnorc.org/projects/Pages/Power-and-Influence-in-Washington.aspx

[3] Congressional approval was 9 percent in November 2013, and in early 2018 hovers around 16 percent. For historical approval trends of Congress, see "Congress and the Public," Gallup, www.gallup.com/poll/1600/congress-public.aspx

[4] For three retirement speeches laced with worry over our representative system, see Mike DeBonis, "Rep. Charlie Dent, Outspoken GOP Moderate, Will Not Seek Reelection," *Washington Post*, September 07, 2017. www.washingtonpost.com/news/powerpost/wp/2017/09/07/rep-charlie-dent-outspoken-gop-moderate-will-not-seek-reelection/?tid=a_inl&utm_term=.a1fbba322114; Maxwell Tani, "John Boehner Just Gave an Emotional Last Speech," *Business Insider*, October 29, 2015, www.businessinsider.com/john-boehner-last-speech-2015-10; and Aaron Blake, "President Obama's Farewell Speech Transcript, Annotated," *Washington Post*, January 10, 2017, www.washingtonpost.com/news/the-fix/wp/2017/01/10/president-obamas-farewell-speech-transcript-annotated/

[5] For more general worries, consider the titles of just a few recent books: Thomas E. Mann and Norman J. Ornstein, *It's Even Worse Than It Looks: How the American Constitutional System Collided with the New Politics of Extremism* (New York: Basic Books, 2016); Adam Garfinkle, *Broken: American Political Dysfunction and What to Do about It* (Washington, DC: American Interest EBooks, 2013); Lawrence Lessig, *Republic Lost: How Money Corrupts Congress – And a Plan to Stop It* (New York: Twelve, 2011); Jacob S. Hacker and Paul Pierson, *Off Center: The Republican Revolution and the Erosion of American Democracy* (New Haven, CT: Yale University Press, 2006); John R. Hibbing and Elizabeth Theiss-Morse, *Congress as Public Enemy: Public Attitudes toward American Political Institutions* (Cambridge: Cambridge University Press, 1995); Larry M. Bartels, *Unequal Democracy: The Political Economy of the New Gilded Age* (Princeton, NJ: Princeton University Press, 2009); and Christopher H. Achen and Larry M. Bartels, *Democracy for Realists: Why Elections Do Not Produce Responsive Government* (Princeton, NJ: Princeton University Press, 2016).

democracy. Many call for returning power to the people via voter initiatives, referenda, and other directly democratic institutions. Others urge going in precisely the opposite direction by insulating policy from politics via technocratic innovations like independent commissions and expert panels. More recently, voters have been drawn to populist candidates who promise to restore the values of some putatively authentic group of their fellow citizens. Finally, "pluralists" believe that previous reform efforts have made the cure worse than the disease, and that we should *strengthen* interest groups, political parties, and the broader apparatus of status quo politics.

We agree that the problems of modern representative democracy are real, but argue that any attempt to double down on establishment politics is likely to deepen the incipient crisis. However, the going reform proposals – direct democracy, technocracy, and reactionary populism – are unlikely to help much either. Each of those proposals misdiagnoses the fundamental problem, and so ends up treating the symptoms rather than the causes of our democratic discontent. Much of that discontent is rooted in the absence of meaningful avenues for citizens to engage in effective dialogue with public officials. As our republic and the complexities of governing it have grown, the Founders' original vision of deliberation oriented toward the commonweal has been narrowed to mean little more than gladiatorial contests between parties and among highly organized interest groups. There is little room for citizens to act in their deliberative capacity *as citizens*, rather than just as consumers. Contemporary democracy asks little more of citizens than their votes and money, and so it is no wonder that many citizens share a sense of dissatisfaction and disconnection from public life.[6]

The great political theorist Hannah Pitkin summed up the problem pointedly:

Representatives act not as agents of the people but simply instead of them. We send them to take care of public affairs like hired experts, and they are professionals, entrenched in office and in party structures. Immersed in a distinct culture of their own, surrounded by other specialists and insulated from the ordinary realities of their constituents' lives ... Their constituents, accordingly, feel powerless and resentful. Having sent experts to tend to their public concerns, they give their own attention and energy to other matters, closer to

---

[6] It is true that protests have ticked up a bit since the Tea Party (on the right) and Indivisible (on the left) have gained momentum. However, disruptive protest is often a poor outlet for deliberation or community building. See Zeynep Tufekci, *Twitter and Tear Gas: The Power and Fragility of Networked Protest* (New Haven, CT: Yale University Press, 2017).

home. Lacking political experience, they feel ignorant and incapable ... Not that people idolize their governors and believe all the official pronouncements. On the contrary, they are cynical and sulky, deeply alienated from what is done in their name and from those who do it ... *The arrangements we call "representative democracy" have become a substitute for popular self-government, not its enactment.*[7]

Our alternative, which we call "directly representative democracy," seeks to reconnect citizens[8] to their government *as citizens* – that is, as partners with their representatives and each other in seeking just and effective policy. On this account, citizens should not be regarded only as consumers who "buy" policy by contributing money to organized interest groups or votes to political parties. Rather, they should have a direct role in advising (*ex ante*) and evaluating (*ex post*) the reasoning and policy actions of their representatives. Thus, we argue that contemporary democracies need new, effective channels of communication between citizens and their government. Rather than merely trying to find the right balance between our representatives acting as "delegates" or "trustees," the goal is to lessen the tension between the two.

In the words of John Adams, representative democracy was rooted in the idea that elected officials should "think, feel, and reason" like the people, often "mixing" with them "and frequently render[ing] to them an account of their stewardship."[9] Adams was right that republican government requires a robust relationship between citizens and their elected officials. Without such contact, politics is at best practiced *for* the people. Critics worry today that it is more often practiced *on* the people. To

---

[7] Hanna Fenichel Pitkin, "Representation and Democracy: Uneasy Alliance," *Scandinavian Political Studies* 27, no. 3 (September 1, 2004): 339. Emphasis added.

[8] Our use of the word "citizen" here and throughout the book raises complicated questions about the proper representative relationship between elected officials and *noncitizens* who live in their electoral jurisdiction. Some countries and localities have experimented with extending voting rights to noncitizens based on the principle of affected interests. And many people would argue that elected officials have specifically representative obligations to noncitizens even in cases where they are not extended the formal franchise. We are certainly open to such arguments, but wish to bracket these questions for purposes of the current study since they require more extended treatment than we can allow for here. We experimented with different ways to address this issue, but decided not to avoid the term "citizen," even when it may not seem precise on some normative interpretations. The reader is encouraged to regard our arguments as applying to anyone they deem to have a legitimate claim on the representational activities of a given elected official.

[9] John Adams, In *The Political Writings of John Adams*, ed. George W. Carey (Washington, DC: Regnery Publishing, 2000), p. 493.

avoid withdrawal or reaction, though, healthy representative democracy requires that elected officials practice politics *with* the people.[10]

To the contemporary observer, the Founders' view may seem naive and outdated. Indeed, some might regard contemporary politics as so bad that such calls for more public discourse go beyond naive into reckless or dangerous. We disagree. We argue that new technologies open up the possibility of repairing the channels of quality communication and the bases of trust between citizens and their representatives. Moreover, our claims are not merely speculative or notional. We base them on the results of our own real-world experiments in democratic innovation. Thirteen sitting members of Congress – themselves frustrated and dissatisfied with status quo politics and the going alternatives – agreed to work with us and groups of their constituents on a set of unprecedented field experiments to test our ideas. We developed new "deliberative town hall" technologies to help strengthen the strained lines of communication and trust with their actual constituents. Political engagement under our innovations was utterly different from the patterns of engagement we see in current practice. Both citizens and their elected representatives behaved differently, and all found the process much more satisfying and constructive than the status quo. The story of those institutional experiments, and what they mean for improving representative democracy, is the story of this book.

A PERFECT STORM

Many citizens believe that establishment politics is nothing but a power game, and a rigged and dubiously rational one at that. They believe that public debate has become completely detached from consultation about the common good with average citizens. And they believe, with some justification, that elected officials listen and respond primarily to powerful special interests. As we will show later in the book, people's perceptions that democracy today reduces to money and votes leads many of them to withdraw from politics, not out of disinterest, but rather out of disgust and despair. And many of those who remain feel like the only outlet for their voices is shouting into the wind. Three interacting trends have combined to make citizens feel like they have little outlet for their voices

---

[10] Our title and discussion here is meant to recall President Lincoln's famous paean to democracy as government of, by, and for the people. Even in Lincoln's time "of" and "by" had to be understood either in an ultimate sense, or perhaps closer to the meaning of "with" that we use, less poetically, here.

other than angry, often bootless protest: the growing size of congressional constituencies; unprecedented levels of party polarization; and a shift in civic organizations away from membership and voice to management and money.

Of course, there have been ways for members of Congress to interact and communicate with constituents since the beginning of the republic. However, these existing opportunities have become strained as congressional constituencies have swelled to several hundred thousand people; as the number of matters the government manages has multiplied; and as policy problems have grown more complex. Contemporary Washington politics is now almost exclusively the domain of media-savvy legislators, highly trained committee staff, legal counsel, agency heads, lobbyists, and expert policy analysts. Today, it is difficult for interested citizens even to understand the policy process, much less have their voices heard in it.[11] As a consequence, citizens are disengaged from – and distressed by – the work of Congress.

Alas, the citizens who remain engaged tend to be more extreme politically, view their partisan opponents with greater antipathy, and are less interested in deliberative communication than citizens a generation ago.[12] Such a dynamic can set off a self-reinforcing cycle, as politics becomes even more polarized and bitterly partisan. As one former senator argued:

The structure of governing isn't working ... [Members of Congress] are all a product of what comes out of their town meetings ... It pulls them to the right or pulls them to the left, and it imposes a huge penalty if they decide they want to be somebody that wants to meet in the middle someplace.[13]

Indeed, the two major parties in the United States have been growing more polarized over the last forty years, and are now more so than at any time since the modern party system emerged. This process aggravates the problems with deliberative voice created by the longer-term trend toward larger constituencies since the size of the House of Representatives was fixed in 1910, and the franchise was (rightly) extended in 1920 and 1971. Figure I.1

---

[11] Hugh Heclo, "Issue Networks and the Executive Establishment," In *The New American Political System*, ed. Anthony King (American Enterprise Institute, 1978), 87–124.

[12] Samantha Smith, "A Wider Ideological Gap between More and Less Educated Adults," *Pew Research Center for the People and the Press*, April 26, 2016, www.people-press .org/2016/04/26/a-wider-ideological-gap-between-more-and-less-educated-adults/

[13] Jennifer Steinhauer and David M. Herszenhorn, "Congress Recesses, Leaving More Stalemates Than Accomplishments," *New York Times*, July 14, 2016, www.nytimes .com/2016/07/15/us/politics/congress-recesses-leaving-more-stalemates-than-accomplishments.html

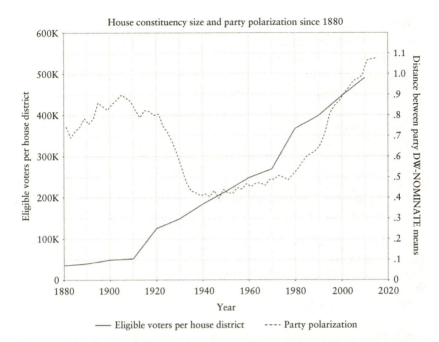

FIGURE I.1. *The voting eligible population of congressional districts continues to increase (solid line) at the same time that partisan polarization (dotted line) has sharply increased post-1980*

shows the relationship between both district size (solid line) and partisan polarization (dotted line) since 1880. We measure district size using the average count of eligible voters per district, and we measure partisan polarization based on the ideological distance between Democratic and Republican members of Congress.[14]

Figure I.1 reveals three broad eras in American politics since 1880. Prior to 1940 Congress was highly polarized but Congressional districts were relatively small. Congressional districts increased steadily in size between 1940 and 1980 but that was also a time of relatively low partisan polarization. Starting around 1980, however, the two trends dramatically coincide and create the circumstances for much of the disaffection citizens feel toward contemporary representative democracy.

[14] Voteview, https://voteview.com. Distance is in terms of the widely used DW-NOMINATE score, derived from a statistical procedure that uses the voting records of members of Congress to give a number for how liberal or conservative each member votes over time. Our measure of partisan polarization in Figure 1.1 shows the distance between the average DW-NOMINATE score for Democrat and Republican members.

Worse yet, these trends in partisanship and formal representation also coincide with fewer meaningful opportunities for exercising political voice in civil society. As Theda Skocpol documents,[15] over the last forty years such organizations have moved dramatically from a "membership" to a "management" model of representing both general and special interests:

> The very model of civic effectiveness has been upended since the 1960s. No longer do civic entrepreneurs think of constructing vast federations and recruiting interactive citizen-members. When a new cause (or tactic) arises, activists envisage opening a national office and managing association-building as well as national projects from the center. Even a group aiming to speak for large numbers of Americans does not absolutely need members. And if mass adherents are recruited through the mail, why hold meetings? From a managerial point of view, interactions with groups of members may be downright inefficient. In the old-time membership federations, annual elections of leaders and a modicum of representative governance went hand in hand with membership dues and interactive meetings. But for the professional executives of today's advocacy organizations, direct mail members can be more appealing because ... "they contribute without meddling" and "do not take part in leadership selection or policy discussions."

That is to say, excluding deliberative participation appears to be a feature, not a bug, in evolving interest-group liberalism. In Skocpol's view, it is (paradoxically) the groups most committed to advocating for some greater purpose that are most likely to conceive of their "members" as primarily check-writers.

We believe that our reform proposals would be valuable in lessening the back and forth tension between direct democracy and elite representation under any circumstances. But the combination of these three trends makes it an especially crucial moment to augment the deliberative capacity of representative institutions.

BEYOND POPULISTS, PLANNERS, AND PLEBISCITES

Against this backdrop, it is not surprising that so many citizens have seen fit to simply withdraw from institutions of representative democracy. But giving up on representative democracy is giving up on a lot, so some have turned their thoughts to reform proposals. Jeremiads against dysfunctional establishment politics come with calls for reform that fall into three basic varieties: direct democracy, technocracy, or populist leadership.

---

[15] Theda Skocpol, *Diminished Democracy: From Membership to Management in American Civic Life* (Norman, OK: University of Oklahoma Press, 2013).

Direct democratic reformers seek to make representative democracy less representative, with calls for returning power directly to the people via referenda, initiatives, and recalls. Technocratic reformers move in exactly the opposite direction, arguing for more insulation of policy from democratic politics – for example, independent commissions, weak parties, strong bureaucracies, or governance by policy experts. Finally, those looking for populist leadership are attracted to strong executives who promise to bypass the messy, putatively debased process of normal legislation.

Each of these three approaches may have its merits, but none goes to the root of the problem of modern representative democracy. For example, recent experiences in California and other states that make heavy use of voter initiatives and referenda suggest that directly democratic policy-making, ironically, may be even more subject to the influence of money, cooptation, and special interests than normal legislative politics.[16] The massive costs of getting an issue onto the ballot, as well as advertising and lobbying for it, mean that powerful, well-financed groups use it as a tool to advance their special interests, despite the patina of popular control. Moreover, the piecemeal nature of initiatives can lead to less coherent policy relative to broad party agendas.[17] For example, initiatives limiting taxation have made it impossible to implement reforms of prisons, schools, and infrastructure that have also garnered clear popular support.[18]

Few citizens have the time or resources to read and analyze the technical details of referenda directly and thoroughly. Indeed, they may not even have the inclination: much of the apparent enthusiasm for direct democratic measures stems from a desire to avoid the perceived corruption of establishment politics rather than real enthusiasm for direct measures. Moreover, critics worry that standard directly democratic practices fail to be even minimally deliberative, since they completely cut out legislative deliberation and the broader conversation that formal debate stimulates.[19] It is worth repeating the old saw

---

[16] Bruce E. Cain, *Democracy More or Less: America's Political Reform Quandary* (Cambridge: Cambridge University Press, 2014); Michael A. Neblo, "Reform Pluralism as Political Theology and Democratic Technology," *Election Law Journal* 13, no. 4 (2014): 526–33.

[17] Nancy L. Rosenblum, *On the Side of the Angels: An Appreciation of Parties and Partisanship* (Princeton, NJ: Princeton University Press, 2008).

[18] Elisabeth R. Gerber et al., *Stealing the Initiative: How State Government Responds to Direct Democracy. Real Politics in America* (Upper Saddle River, NJ: Prentice Hall, 2001).

[19] John R. Hibbing and Elizabeth Theiss-Morse, *Stealth Democracy: Americans' Beliefs about How Government Should Work* (Cambridge: Cambridge University Press, 2002);

that direct majorities are just as capable of tyranny – both gross and mundane – as less direct forms of government.[20] For all of these reasons, then, reformers who propose to reduce the role of representation in representative government cannot solve the core problems facing modern democracies.

Worries over the problems endemic to direct democracy motivate some reformers to try the inverse tack. Technocratic innovations – such as independent commissions, central banks, autonomous bureaucracies, and the like – seek to insulate policy from both establishment politics and the vicissitudes of direct democracy. However, such attempts often end up foundering on so-called democratic deficits.[21] Many citizens say that they want policy to be removed from the messy process of standard politics, which they view as corrupt and irrational. They long for experts who will simply execute the policies that "everyone" already knows are in the common interest, only to find that the experts often disagree with them and indeed often cannot arrive at a consensus among themselves. On some issues, such as military base closings, elected officials are happy to comply, so that they can avoid taking no-win public stands. Independent commissions and other attempts to insulate the policy process provide political cover. But the process is seldom so simple and is prone to backfire. When citizens perceive that their voices are not being heard in the policy process – an almost built-in feature of technocracy – normal imperfections in policy outcomes become magnified, decreasing confidence in political institutions.[22] Protests against "unaccountable" central banks and the Brexit backlash against European Union bureaucracy are but two examples.

Robert A. Dahl, *Democracy and Its Critics* (New Haven, CT: Yale University Press, 1992); James S. Fishkin, *Democracy and Deliberation: New Directions for Democratic Reform* (New Haven, CT: Yale University Press, 1991).

[20] "The Federalist #55," Accessed February 24, 2017. www.constitution.org/fed/federa55.htm. Madison argues that, "In all very numerous assemblies, of whatever character composed, passion never fails to wrest the scepter from reason. Had every Athenian citizen been a Socrates, every Athenian assembly would still have been a mob."

[21] Pippa Norris, *Democratic Deficit: Critical Citizens Revisited* (Cambridge: Cambridge University Press, 2011).

[22] Joy L. Pritts et al., "Veterans' Views on Balancing Privacy and Research in Medicine: A Deliberative Democratic Study," *Michigan State University Journal of Medicine and Law* 12 (2008): 17. Beyond matters of public perception, depoliticized policy formation is acutely subject to regulatory capture, magnifying the influence of special interests. While experts typically have superior technical knowledge about a policy area, there is no reason to believe that their value judgments will be superior to those of the public. Michael E. Levine and Jennifer L. Forrence, "Regulatory Capture, Public Interest, and the Public Agenda: Toward a Synthesis," *Journal of Law, Economics, & Organization* 6 (1990): 167–98.

If direct democratic and technocratic reforms attempt to weaken (respectively) the representative and democratic aspects of representative democracy, reactionary populists attempt to strengthen both, but in the peculiar sense of embodying the will of the people in the will of a strong leader. Like direct democrats and technocrats, populists regard status quo politics as the province of a corrupt and self-serving elite who have become detached from "the people." The remedy, however, is to consolidate power in the hands of an uncorrupted and selfless executive who can bypass the messiness of the normal legislative process.

Alas, history shows that it is difficult to find executives who stay immune to corruption, are selfless, and genuinely embody the whole of diverse societies in a single person. Even just at the policy level, such executives often promise more than they can deliver, or worse, deliver "results" at the cost of running roughshod over social diversity and the checks and balances of democratic governance. Either they get caught in a downward spiral of legitimacy akin to the original disaffection with status quo politics, or they damage the liberal restraints of modern representative democracy. Italian and German fascists arose originally as populist nationalists via fairly standard institutions of representative democracy. Less disastrous, if still worrisome, examples abound in the nationalist movements sweeping the globe. Reactionary populism, though tempting, rarely ends up solving the problems of representative democracy at their root.

One of the core challenges of modern representative democracy consists in the citizenry developing and maintaining warranted trust in their elected officials despite the enormous growth in constituency size, party polarization, and the complexity of governance. When the public loses confidence in establishment politics, the polity ends up lurching between perceived remedies (populists, planners, and plebiscites) that fail to restore confidence, do little to ameliorate citizens' sense of alienation from their government, and generate commensurate problems of their own.

Dissatisfaction with the perceived excesses of direct, technocratic, and populist reforms has even led to a backlash, with some arguing that we should reinforce the role of political parties and interest groups – the elite-driven system of government that political scientists refer to as "pluralism." To many modern-day pluralists, citizens today are petulant and unrealistic "politiphobes," directing their anger at the intrinsic limits of modern representative democracy.[23] As one observer notes:

[23] Jonathan Rauch, "How American Politics Went Insane." *Atlantic*, July, 2016, http://people.ucls.uchicago.edu/~cjuriss/US/Documents/US-Jurisson-How-American-Politics

Washington doesn't have a crisis of leadership; it has a crisis of followership ... Congress's incompetence makes the electorate even more disgusted, which leads to even greater political volatility. In a Republican presidential debate in March, Ohio Governor John Kasich described the cycle this way: The people, he said, "want change, and they keep putting outsiders in to bring about the change. Then the change doesn't come ... because we're putting people in that don't understand compromise." Disruption in politics and dysfunction in government reinforce each other. Chaos becomes the new normal. Being a disorder of the [body politic's] immune system, chaos syndrome magnifies other problems, turning political head colds into pneumonia.[24]

From the pluralist perspective, citizens should accept that the political establishment is the only game in town.

A simple return to establishment politics, however, will not solve the root problem underlying citizens' growing sense of alienation from politics, since it would fail to address the way that size and complexity strain channels of communication and trust between citizens and their representatives. Doing so will only perpetuate the cycle that demobilized and demoralized average citizens in the first place. Doubling down on interest group and party politics, then, will only aggravate the very problems that we began with. If so, then it might appear that there is no way to expand the capacities of representative democracy, and thus our only option is to sensibly blend and balance the going reform proposals with status quo politics.

We argue, however, that contemporary disaffection with politics is *internally* related to what citizens see as the failures of status quo politics as interest group pluralism and partisan bloodsport.[25] Current patterns of engagement do not necessarily reflect how most citizens would engage with elected officials given more attractive opportunities. Pluralists and establishment reformers alike falsely assume that citizens who do not even bother to vote would not want to participate in a more demanding form of democracy that requires increased time and cognitive effort.[26] We offer a demonstration to the contrary.

-Became-So-Ineffective-Atlantic-2016–07.pdf; Cain, *Democracy More or Less: America's Political Reform Quandary*; Rosenblum, *On the Side of the Angels: An Appreciation of Parties and Partisanship*; and Achen and Bartels, *Democracy for Realists: Why Elections Do Not Produce Responsive Government*.

[24] Rauch, "How American Politics Went Insane."

[25] Hibbing and Theiss-Morse, *Stealth Democracy: Americans' Beliefs about How Government Should Work*.

[26] Michael A. Neblo et al., "Who Wants to Deliberate – And Why?," *The American Political Science Review* 104, no. 3 (August 2010): 566–83.

DIRECTLY REPRESENTATIVE DEMOCRACY

The fundamental problem in contemporary democracy is that the representative relationship between citizens and elected officials has become strained in such a way that citizens no longer trust that their individual voices are being heard and heeded. At best they take up a posture of angry, demanding customers. Representation has become almost exclusively the representation of interests, rather than the representation of people.

While elements of direct, technocratic, populist, and even pluralist reform initiatives may have their place, we argue that a much more broadly promising reform paradigm has been overlooked: *directly representative democracy*. Directly representative democracy is a proposal for building more direct, inclusive and deliberative connections between citizens and government officials in order to create alternatives to our broken system of interest group politics and blind partisanship. We propose it as a paradigm to narrow the gap between our highest ideals and disappointing realities by leveraging new communication technologies to reconnect citizens to their "immediate representatives."

Political theorists and political reformers have traditionally contrasted direct and representative democracy, depending upon how much power is exercised directly by the people themselves (e.g., in referenda) versus how mediated that exercise is through representatives (e.g., via elected officials). We claim that the traditional contrast between direct and representative democracy – at least as it plays out in today's discussions about political reform – does not fully capture the practical possibilities. We propose augmenting existing democratic institutions to make them simultaneously both more direct *and* more representative. Doing so will enable citizens to reconnect with their representatives, engaging them in important, substantive policy matters.

Directly representative institutions can take many forms, and can connect citizens with any branch of government. Our own innovation in directly representative democracy involves a new kind of online deliberative town hall meeting that brings average citizens into dialogue with their elected legislators on important policy matters, *directly as citizens*, rather than only as voters, campaign contributors, or members of interest groups. Both the citizens and the members of Congress who participated in our project agreed that the deliberative town hall that we designed improves communication and trust.[27] Thus, our term, *directly*

---

[27] It is important to note that we do not regard our deliberative town halls as the only institutional innovation available under directly representative democracy. Our paradigm

representative democracy, is not an oxymoron, nor merely some middle position between direct and representative democracy. Rather it *expands* the policy-making and legitimacy-evoking capacities of representative democracy itself.[28] The core ideas behind directly representative democracy are simple and intuitive.

Our approach is *direct* in that the primary representative relationship is between a constituent and her elected official. Parties and interest groups, though important, are emphatically secondary and derivative. You may be an environmentalist, an evangelical Christian, a Teamster, a Republican, or some combination of these. The representative claim that you have on your elected officials, however, does not depend upon and need not flow through these identities. Direct representation in this sense is important for both theoretical and practical reasons. Theoretically, we are all individual citizens with rights and the moral power of political judgment – something that is not merely a weighted average of our supposed group interests and identities. Moreover, when those characteristics are translated into the policy process, they often get used in a misguided way. Say that you are an environmentalist, and as such, you are leery of genetically modified foods. But you do not like pesticides either, and GMOs require fewer pesticides. And you are worried that without either, food costs will go up, causing hardship for poor people, contrary to your egalitarian commitments. Such cross-cutting identities create cross-cutting frames and considerations that inform our political judgments. But interest groups (including *public* interest groups) tend to act as inflexible agents of their core demands. Direct representation ameliorates this problem, and encourages citizens to engage policy in a more substantive and nuanced way.[29]

Our approach is *representative* in that it focuses on and seeks to improve citizen communication within institutions of representative government, rather than emphasizing initiatives, referenda and other unmediated institutions as the primary engines of reform. Directly representative democracy agrees that the scale and scope of modern democracies preclude direct institutions from effectively serving as more than a

---

offers a way of thinking about the core problems of representative democracy that have many implications, which we discuss in our concluding chapter.

[28] Michael A. Neblo, "Deliberation's Legitimation Crisis," *Critical Review* 23, no. 3 (2011): 405–19.

[29] One promising new online platform that enables participants to explore the nuances of complex problems is the Common Ground for Action (CGA) forum developed by the Kettering Foundation and National Issues Forum Institute.

supplement in governance. Unlike the relatively few enfranchised citizens of ancient Athens, most citizens of contemporary democracies have day jobs and many other demands on their time. The benefits of representative government, moreover, are not merely matters of "second best." Talented public servants who acquire policy expertise can promote high quality deliberation, develop coherent and forward-looking policy, and protect against lurches in public opinion, among other reasons to favor representative over direct democracy.[30]

Our approach is *democratic* in that we seek to create new and meaningful opportunities for citizens to participate in ways that go beyond checking off a ballot every few years, writing a check to a political organization, or shouting protest slogans. Indeed, our vision is closer to the civics textbook presentation of democracy than either technocracy or interest group pluralism. Directly representative democracy centers on reintroducing effective and inclusive communication between citizen and legislators.

Thus, directly representative democracy is direct in that it bypasses and supplements the highly mediated pathways via interest groups, parties, and mass media that constitute status quo politics. It is representative in that it strengthens established representative institutions rather than attempting to work around them. And it is democratic in that citizens play a robust role through all phases of the political process, rather than simply showing up every four years to render an up or down judgment.

Effective communication, of course, is a two-way street. Officials should communicate the reasons for their actions to constituents; but they must also genuinely listen to their constituents. Respectful, inclusive, two-way communication helps to establish perceptions of legitimacy and warranted trust in representative democracy. Elected officials build such trust and legitimacy through what we call *ongoing republican consultation* and *ongoing deliberative accountability*.

By *ongoing republican consultation* we mean representatives making special efforts to engage a broad cross-section of their constituents, seeking them out to provide reflective advice and input on substantive policies at the time that policies are under consideration in the legislature. As John Adams noted, representatives must "mix with their constituents" if they are to be able to "think, feel, reason, and act" on their behalf. Contrast republican consultation as envisioned within

---

[30] Kevin M. Esterling, *The Political Economy of Expertise: Information and Efficiency in American National Politics* (Ann Arbor: University of Michigan Press, 2004).

directly representative democracy with politicians' more typical practices of relying merely on electoral mandates, pandering to raw public opinion, attending to vested interests, or attempting to manipulate opinion through "crafted talk."[31] Elections, however, bundle together a large number of issues that constituents care about, making it difficult to interpret democratic support for any given policy proposal. Public opinion polls can sometimes help clarify apparent support on certain issues, but they generally lack anything but the barest of contexts and rationales; moreover, they do not reliably track people's considered views on policy when informed. Nor do they generally lead citizens to feel that they have been "heard" by their representatives in any meaningful way. Finally, when elected officials *do* consult constituencies outside of elections, it tends to be primarily via interest groups, which, we have argued, are a secondary and derivative form of representation. Such an approach does not reliably reflect the way a broader swath of the public would respond if meaningfully consulted.

In a similar vein, by *ongoing deliberative accountability* we mean legislators making special efforts to engage a broad cross-section of their constituents in providing explanations for representative activity throughout the policy process on discrete issues – to "frequently render to them an account of their stewardship" in Adams's words.[32] Our approach encourages accountability between elections, disaggregates issues, and fosters a more deliberative political culture. In one sense, this is merely the flipside of ongoing republican consultation, with an emphasis on legislators explaining how they took such consultation into account in their work. The idea is to expand on the notion of electoral accountability. As we noted above, elections bundle together a large number of issues, with only a few hot-button topics reaching the threshold of attention in compressed and heated campaigns that discourage anything that cannot be crammed into a thirty-second ad designed to contrast maximally with one's opponent. In the context of campaigns, such proposals tend to be long on imagery and short on specifics. As Mario Cuomo noted, "You campaign in poetry; you govern in prose." Citizens should be able to hear and respond to the prose as well.

---

[31] Lawrence R. Jacobs and Robert Y. Shapiro, *Politicians Don't Pander: Political Manipulation and the Loss of Democratic Responsiveness* (Chicago, IL: University of Chicago Press, 2000).

[32] For a related view of accountability see John Adams, In *The Political Writings of John Adams*, ed. George W. Carey (Washington, DC: Regnery Publishing, 2000), p. 493.

When representatives engage in republican consultation and deliberative accountability, they bring citizens into a respectful, two-way discussion that can meaningfully reconnect them to their government. Elected officials have a general duty (and a strong incentive) to enact policies that will eventually be popular among their constituents. However, the officials typically have better information with which to make policy judgments than most citizens, so they do not simply vote for whatever an uninformed public thinks it wants at the moment. They generally do not and should not assume the role of either a paternalistic "trustee" or an effectively direct-democratic "delegate."[33]

Through a system of online deliberative town halls, we envision creating a cycle of deliberation that cuts across this trustee-delegate dichotomy. In this cycle, citizens communicate their general interests, and legislators debate and craft policies to advance those interests via republican consultation. They then attempt to persuade their constituents that they have succeeded via deliberative accountability. The process repeats itself in a cycle of feedback culminating in periodic elections. Directly representative democracy thus breaks out of the zero-sum trade-off between direct and representative democracy. It represents both a theoretical innovation and a practical opportunity, deployable in good times and bad.

The goal of directly representative democracy is to give citizens good reasons to trust that, in ceding some of their sovereign power, they are not also ceding democracy itself. As Mark Twain put it:

In a monarchy, the king and his family are the country; in a republic it is the common voice of the people. Each of you, for himself, by himself and on his own responsibility, must speak. And it is a solemn and weighty responsibility, and not lightly to be flung aside at the bullying of pulpit, press, government, or the empty catch-phrases of politicians.[34]

But why should we believe that politicians – prone as they are to trading in empty catch-phrases – will listen?

---

[33] Hanna Fenichel Pitkin, *The Concept of Representation* (Berkeley: University of California Press, 1967); Brandice Canes-Wrone, *Who Leads Whom?: Presidents, Policy, and the Public* (Chicago, IL: University of Chicago Press, 2010); and Justin Fox and Kenneth W. Shotts, "Delegates or Trustees? A Theory of Political Accountability," *The Journal of Politics* 71, no. 4 (2009): 1225–37.

[34] Mark Twain and John S. Tuckey, *Mark Twain's Fables of Man* (Berkeley: University of California Press, 1972).

TOWNHALLS! (TOWNHALLS?)

We build much of our practical case for *directly representative democracy* with evidence from a series of novel experiments that tested our alternative conception of democracy in a realistic, yet scientifically rigorous way. Members of Congress agreed to participate in our research by hosting specially designed, online deliberative town hall meetings with randomly assigned, representative samples of their constituents, discussing some of the most important and controversial issues of the day – immigration policy and terrorist detainee policy. These experiments demonstrate a model of how our democracy could work, where representatives consult with and inform constituents in substantive discussions, and where otherwise marginalized citizens participate and become empowered.

Town hall meetings are a natural place to start for purposes of trying to enhance two-way dialogue via ongoing republican consultation and deliberative accountability. The modern "town hall meeting" emerged from the classic New England town meeting. Such meetings, with their direct, face-to-face democracy have an iconic status in US history. In his famous "four freedoms" series, Norman Rockwell represents "freedom of speech" in terms of an individual citizen speaking up at a New England town meeting (see the left panel of Figure I.2).

FIGURE I.2. *Rockwell's depiction of a New England town meeting (left) and a photo from one of Obama's town halls (right)*

Recently, members of Congress have used what they call "town hall meetings" to interact with their constituents. Yet these meetings typically fail to promote rational public deliberation very well. Qualitative evidence seems to support the idea that politicians do not typically host town hall meetings to engage in discussion on the merits of issues and controversies. Rather, the highly unusual types of constituents who attend these face-to-face meetings lead representatives to use the platform primarily to rally their strongest supporters and to deflect the attacks of their most vocal opponents.[35]

The 2009 and 2017 town halls on, respectively, enacting health care reform and then its possible repeal, for example, suggest that whatever semblance of reality Rockwell's portrait may have captured has been almost entirely lost. The health care town halls routinely devolved into shouting matches interspersed with threatened and, occasionally, actual violence. The armed man in the right panel seems as if he might be the radicalized grandson of the genial citizen in the left panel.[36]

Technocratic reformers and those who want to reinforce status quo politics may be apt to think that, in focusing on town halls, we have chosen the least plausible venue to argue in favor of directly representative reforms. On this account, town halls are emblematic of exactly what is wrong with trying to incorporate average citizens into the political and policy process, and any attempt to expand their scope and influence is at best a waste of time, at worst a recipe for disaster.

INSTITUTIONAL DESIGN

Such concerns are reasonable. We do not advocate a return to some Rockwellian golden age. Yet, as we argued above, directly representative democracy is designed to promote something like most people's civics textbook vision of how democracy is supposed to work, with citizens directly and constructively engaging with their representatives. We teach children this vision because it embodies our deepest ideals and

---

[35] Jane J. Mansbridge, *Beyond Adversary Democracy* (Chicago, IL: University of Chicago Press, 1983); Richard F. Fenno, *Home Style: House Members in Their Districts* (Boston, MA: Little, Brown and Co., 1978); and Smith, "A Wider Ideological Gap between More and Less Educated Adults."

[36] The sign the man holds refers to Jefferson's famous words: "The tree of liberty must be refreshed from time to time with the blood of patriots & tyrants." See also: Christopher F. Karpowitz and Chad Raphael, *Deliberation, Democracy, and Civic Forums: Improving Equality and Publicity* (Cambridge: Cambridge University Press, 2014).

commitments. We should be slow to toss it aside even in the face of seemingly intractable problems. As Max Weber noted, "politics is a strong and slow boring of hard boards."

We began this project, then, with a simple conjecture – that the worrisome spectacle of many standard town halls was largely a result of who shows up: either very politically active citizens who already love their member of Congress or those who are nursing specific grievances – i.e., their most vocal critics.[37] The vast majority of each representative's constituents fall into *neither* camp. Generalizing from what happens in the ensuing discussions in the standard town halls may be wildly inaccurate relative to what would transpire if town halls could be designed to encourage widespread, informed, and constructive participation.

Relatively small changes to the institutional structure behind town halls would encourage broader and higher quality participation. As it turns out, the main reason that citizens do not participate in political events outside of voting is that no one asks them to do so. Simply asking people to participate can dramatically increase the rate and representativeness of those who show up, as does using online technology to lower the costs of participation.[38] As we shall see, changing who shows up profoundly changes how events unfold. Making deliberative participation much easier is realistic with moderate effort on the part of elected representatives. We therefore see it as both a positive duty of outreach as well as an increasingly prudent and plausible communication strategy for elected officials.

REAL(ISTIC) POLITICS

When we first started presenting work from this project, people often responded with comments like, "Wow, those experiments with online town halls are really cool. Of course, they're not real politics." They questioned whether directly representative outreach really is an increasingly prudent and plausible activity for elected officials. Yet the deliberative town halls we have already put into practice involved *sitting* members of Congress talking with their *actual* constituents about *real* legislation. If

---

[37] See Smith, "A Wider Ideological Gap between More and Less Educated Adults."

[38] Fay Lomax Cook, Michael X. Delli Carpini, and Lawrence R. Jacobs. "Who Deliberates? Discursive Participation in America," In *Deliberation, Participation and Democracy: Can the People Govern?*, ed. Shawn W. Rosenberg (London: Palgrave Macmillan, 2007), 25–44; and Neblo et al., "Who Wants to Deliberate – And Why?"

that does not constitute "real" politics, we cannot see why. This may not be politics as usual, but that is the whole point. We are trying to revive a form of politics taken to be essential at the founding of the republic, but that critics now regard as naive given the growth in the size of the country and the complexity of governance.

One might concede that our deliberative town halls were isolated examples of "real" politics, and yet doubt that they can be realistically taken to scale. Can these new institutions of directly representative democracy engage large numbers of citizens or influence elected representatives? The full reply to such concerns will unfold throughout the book, but a few points are worth noting up front. First, in building civic capacity, success breeds success. In our studies as well as studies of jury participation and many other forms of civic engagement, citizens tend to be surprised by how much they like participating, hold on to the gains from doing so, and deploy those gains in new contexts.[39] Because civic participation tends to create a virtuous cycle, the response to the chicken-and-egg problem in building better citizens and better institutions is to start small, but to start somewhere. Creating citizens who are more responsible, prepared, and capable of discharging their roles well requires giving them the means, motives, and opportunities to do so in the first place. Below, we present evidence that many citizens want to engage in an informed and constructive way if they believe that their representatives are not merely putting on a show, that the political process is not irredeemably rigged, and that somebody with power is listening.

Listening, however, is a two-way street, and one may wonder whether the elected officials are actually doing that listening. Can institutions of directly representative democracy really change anything among legislators when the caucus and committee doors close? Although this book emphasizes the effects the deliberative town halls had on citizens rather than on the representatives who participated, there are good reasons to believe that directly representative consultation can influence elected officials as well. In addition to electoral goals, elected officials have governance goals, and the *informed* views of their constituents will typically influence their judgments about good governance.

Since V. O. Key, political scientists have also argued that elected officials care about *latent* opinion – that is, public opinion that will emerge

---

[39] John Gastil, Chiara Bacci, and Michael Dollinger, "Is Deliberation Neutral? Patterns of Attitude Change during 'The Deliberative Polls™'," *Journal of Public Deliberation* 6, no. 2 (2010): Article 3.

after the official takes some action. Standard public opinion surveys are not reliable indicators of future or emerging public opinion because most people do not pay much attention to legislation outside the context of election campaigns. Ongoing republican consultation, however, is likely to yield a form of deliberative opinion that better tracks latent opinion among constituents. Thus, elected officials and parties can use republican consultation to avoid mistakes that they themselves might later regret.

For their part, citizens can make two kinds of mistakes regarding the actions of their representatives. They can support actions that they would not have approved had they been better informed, and they can fail to support actions that they would have supported. Directly representative democratic reforms seek to minimize such mistakes by placing citizens in a better position to both inform and judge their representatives. Informed citizens, then, give the representatives better information and better incentives to make good choices, and enable them to convincingly communicate, in turn, the grounds for those choices to their constituents. By building new ways for legislators and citizens to interact constructively, directly representative democracy aspires to help reconnect citizens to their government, thus improving democratic outcomes. We present the evidence for each step in this process below.

In the next chapter we develop our vision and aspirations for directly democratic institutions, proposing a list of five normative criteria that any successful reform effort should meet. Chapter 2 describes the institutional design of our deliberative town halls. In Chapters 3 through 7 we assess how well our deliberative town halls measured up to our five criteria. In the conclusion, we reflect on our experiment and consider the prospects for directly representative democracy going forward.

I

The Spirit and Form of Popular Government

To secure the public good and private rights against the danger of faction, and at the same time to preserve the spirit and the form of popular government, is then the great object to which our inquiries are directed.

—James Madison, Federalist 10

The American founders were clear-eyed about power politics, yet sought a form of government that aspired to go beyond simply channeling and controlling power. Since that time many have come to see interest-group politics and implacable partisanship as simply what democratic politics is, and thus talk of orienting politics toward the public good as naive at best. Yet Madison's highest aspiration was to secure the public good *against* factional interests, and to do so while preserving "the spirit and form of popular government."

As noted earlier, none of the going reform paradigms secure all of Madison's conditions simultaneously. Interest group pluralism effectively surrenders to faction. Technocracy retreats from popular government. Populism has a poor track record of protecting basic rights. And direct democracy no more reliably conduces to the common good than the going alternatives, with scale typically preventing adequate scope for deliberation. Our best hope for reform, then, is to improve the institutions of representative democracy.

Our inquiries here are thus directed to the same great object as Madison, even if our ambitions are more modest. Madison famously argued that there was no *cure* for the mischiefs of faction, or at least none that did not abrogate our liberties. We can only manage and mitigate the *symptoms*. By "faction" he meant groups that promoted their interests over the common good or the rights of others. In The Federalist #10, Madison reasoned that no sensible reform proposal can wish away conflicting interests or deny people the right to organize themselves to petition government to advance their interests. Instead, an "extended republic" with sufficiently diverse interests would create a setting where no one interest could be a stable majority, and so interest groups could be a check on each others' power. There will always be interest-group politics, but that does not mean that all politics should reduce to interest groups. Individual citizens have interests but that does not mean interest groups alone can adequately represent those citizens in all of their complexity.

Both the quest for the public good and the spirit and form of popular government imply that we must foster institutional alternatives to pure interest-group politics. From the time of the founding, the individualist strain in American political thought has been balanced by a more "republican" strain emphasizing the virtue and vigilance of active citizens engaging their government about the common good.[1]

Adams and Madison may strike some as naive today. Indeed, historically speaking it was easier for the Founders to assume that citizens (or at least the citizens they had in mind) could connect with the government in deliberative interactions. The nation was much smaller, the franchise much more restricted, and the scope of problems to be debated much narrower. Thus, Madison helped to solve the problem of faction for his time, but he did not anticipate the emergent problems of deliberation in an extended republic on anywhere near the scale that we face today. In particular, he could not have envisioned the extent to which factions in modern, large republics, dominated by parties and interest groups, would progressively crowd out deliberation in civic life and representative institutions. Directly representative democracy helps solve the problem of deliberation in a modern, extended republic.

INVESTING IN OUR DELIBERATIVE INFRASTRUCTURE

We argue that much of the disillusionment with contemporary democracy is rooted in a continuing imbalance between the many institutional

---

[1] Consider John Adams's warning against an excessive emphasis on "the spirit of commerce" and the interest-group politics that it fostered: "Public virtue is the only foundation of republics. There must be a positive passion for the public good, the public interest ... established in the minds of the people, or there can be no republican government, nor any real liberty: and this public passion must be superior to all private passions." John Adams, "John Adams to Mercy Otis Warren," April 16, 1776, Accessed May 28, 2018. https://founders.archives.gov/documents/Adams/06–04-02-0044.

channels for asserting private interests and the few channels for deliberating about the public good. As with our roads and bridges, the communicative infrastructure supporting our democracy needs to be upgraded.

Of course, there are existing opportunities for citizens to connect their voices directly to politics and to their representatives in Congress – for example, constituent mail or standard in-person town hall meetings. But the infrastructure for such exchanges is currently not developed well enough for these channels to realize much of their deliberative potential. Congressional offices are overwhelmed by constituent mail, much of it mass-mailings organized by interest groups with little deliberative content, and from highly skewed portions of the constituency. As a result, answering mail has become merely a kind of constituent service, a task delegated to college interns, rather than powerfully influencing the legislative work of representatives.[2] Nor, as we discuss more extensively below, do standard in-person town halls tend to be very consultative or constructive.

Directly representative democracy, through the vehicle of a deliberative town hall, provides a new channel of communication to foster citizens' direct and deliberative engagement with their representatives. Its goal is to lessen the tension between direct democracy and representation. Representative democracy recommends itself over direct democracy in part because policy should not simply reflect the raw, possibly uninformed, or hastily considered preferences of the mass public. Direct democracy recommends itself over representative forms in part because policy should be responsive to the judgments and wishes of the citizenry in some robust sense. Directly representative practices encourage mass preferences to be less raw, less purely individualistic, less ambiguous, and more thoroughly considered. At the same time, they encourage more, and more sensible, responsiveness among elected officials to considered public judgment.[3]

With this approach we need not focus on rendering interest group conflict itself deliberative. Instead, we need to build and reinforce new, more direct institutional channels within the deliberative system that bypass the main flow of power under interest group pluralism.[4] Rebalancing republican

---

[2] Communicating with Congress: How Citizen Advocacy Is Changing Mail Operations on Capitol Hill (Washington, DC: Congressional Management Foundation, 2011).

[3] Madison famously believed that scale could actually *help* with the problem of faction, though it is not clear that he would have argued that such benefit was strictly increasing across the range from then to now. Moreover, our argument is that he certainly did not anticipate the way that his solution for faction would crowd out deliberation, another key good that he was trying to promote.

[4] For more background on the concept of the deliberative system used here, see Michael Neblo, "Thinking through Democracy: Between the Theory and Practice of Deliberative

and interest-based politics will yield the most benefit not by cutting out interest groups and political parties completely, but by opening up and supporting direct lines of communication as alternative paths to connecting the reasoning of citizens and elected officials. Such paths will be valuable only to the extent that they foster constructive two-way communication. Politicians' Twitter accounts create a kind of unmediated connection between representatives and constituents, but the medium is not two-way. It also seems not to elevate the quality of discourse in the public sphere.

Over the last thirty years, deliberative democrats have sought to revive the republican emphasis on an orientation toward public reasoning about the public good, while integrating it with realistic elements of representative democracy and interest group politics. At the heart of deliberative democracy lies a theory of political legitimacy in which people who disagree over policies exchange reasons about "what we should do" (as opposed to "what I want"). Engaging in such two-way communication seeks to establish common ground on points of agreement, generate fresh perspectives, foster respect for opposing views, and ultimately invest the democratic process itself with legitimacy. Such a deliberative exchange involves a process of discovery, where those involved in the discussion can "refine and enlarge" their initial opinions regarding good public policy.[5]

Scholars have developed a vast literature on deliberative democracy with many variations in emphasis. We opt for a fairly minimal definition that is compatible with most of those variations. For our purposes, then, deliberative democracy can be defined as:

A form of government in which free and equal citizens (and their representatives), justify decisions in a process in which they give one another reasons that are generally accessible, with the aim of reaching conclusions that are binding in the present but open to challenge in the future.[6]

From this compact statement we can derive several criteria for institutional reform that would be recognizable to almost all theories of deliberative democracy and that can serve as a measuring stick for evaluating

Politics," *Acta Politica* 40, no. 2 (2005): 169–81; and Michael A. Neblo, *Deliberative Democracy between Theory and Practice* (Cambridge: Cambridge University Press, 2015).

5 For a fuller discussion, see Joshua Cohen, "Deliberation and Democratic Legitimacy," in *The Good Polity,* ed. Alan Hamlin and Philip Pettit (New York: Basil Blackwell, 1989), 17–34.

6 Amy Gutmann and Dennis Thompson, *Why Deliberative Democracy?* (Princeton, NJ: Princeton University Press, 2004), 7.

reform proposals. We introduce these criteria here and will elaborate on them below. First, *inclusion:* institutional reforms should proceed in a way that promotes equality and inclusivity among citizens in the process. Second, *informed justification:* to justify the decisions the process should proceed on the basis of the best available and carefully balanced information. Third, *good reason-giving:* the process should embody high quality reason-giving. Fourth, *promoting legitimacy:* to justify binding decisions, the process should foster legitimacy and trust in the process. Fifth and finally, *scalability:* the deliberative process should work on such a scale that it can affect the larger political system.

Rather than simply having everyone cut their best deal and letting the chips fall where they may – as with interest-group pluralism – deliberative democrats want to make us accountable to each other in a way that typically goes beyond justifying our choices merely by saying "That is what I want." As a result, unlike many other approaches linking empirical research to democratic theory, we do not take responsiveness to pre-given (possibly uninformed and poorly considered) preferences as the key evaluative criterion.

No theory of deliberative democracy could or should do without the institutions of interest-group and partisan politics. Yet developing directly representative institutions will help to rebalance status quo politics with republican elements. The best opportunity for improvement centers on creating new institutions, such as the deliberative town hall, that encourage citizens to interact with their representatives *as* citizens, rather than solely as members of political parties or organized factions. We demonstrate that citizens have both the capacity and the desire to engage with their elected officials in this more substantive way. We argue as well that elected officials have strong incentives to genuinely engage their constituents via direct representation in order to cultivate trust in and regard for their work as officeholders.[7]

WHAT MIGHT DIRECTLY REPRESENTATIVE DEMOCRACY LOOK LIKE?

In the introduction we previewed the deliberative town halls that will be the focus of our empirical investigation below. But one can imagine many other nominees for directly representative democracy in the broader deliberative system. The principles behind directly representative

---

[7] Fenno, *Home Style: House Members in Their Districts.*

democracy as a reform paradigm recommend experimenting with much more than just town halls. Deliberative democrats have proposed and experimented with many new institutions such as the Oregon Citizen Initiative Review, parliamentary chambers selected by lot, participatory budgeting, Deliberative Polls, and citizen juries, among others. Most of these ideas have much to recommend them. Yet most focus on increasing the directness of democracy itself rather than on the directness of *representation* within democracy.

For example, to increase directly representative democracy one could design more formally institutionalized deliberation *within* political parties: first between average members and rank-and-file officials, and then aggregating up to interactions between the rank-and-file and party leadership. Such an arrangement might be especially useful in adapting directly representative reform opportunities into party-list, multi-party, and high party discipline systems. Indeed, the recent Irish constitutional reform and several initiatives from India's reformist Aam Aadmi Party can be interpreted productively in terms of directly representative democracy.[8]

Even staying within the US context, however, the principles behind directly representative democracy recommend experimenting with other potential reforms both within government itself, and more broadly within the political system. One could easily adapt our ideas and practices to consultation at the level of state or local government, or in fulfilling "maximal public input" requirements for bureaucratic agencies. In the context of civic associations and interest groups, directly representative principles recommend a return to once-common consultative practices within such organizations. These practices have faded with the alienating trend of such organizations treating their members as mere resources to be managed, rather than participants to be heeded.[9]

---

[8] For example, the AAP conducted the "Delhi Dialogue" as a form of constituent consultation about policies to bridge the digital divide, in an effort to enable even greater reach for such online consultation. See Rekha Diwakar, "Local contest, national impact: understanding the success of India's Aam Aadmi Party in 2015 Delhi assembly election," *Representation* 52, no. 1 (2016): 71–80. In addition, "All of Delhi's [AAP] Ministers are fully accessible to the public without appointment at their official residences between 10am and 11am every morning from Monday to Friday." On the Irish constitutional co-deliberations between citizens and elected officials, see Jane Suiter, David Farrell, and Clodagh Harris, "The Irish Constitutional Convention: A Case of 'High Legitimacy'?" in *Constitutional Deliberative Democracy in Europe*, ed. Min Reuchamps and Jane Suiter (London, UK: ECPR Press, 2016), 33–52.

[9] Skocpol, *Diminished Democracy: From Membership to Management in American Civic Life*.

That said, we argue that the most important path in the deliberative system currently in need of reform is the one connecting legislators with the citizens that they represent. We focus on this path rather than other potential reform opportunities because we believe that it is the one in most critical need of repair. It is also a path for which we have assembled experimental evidence as a proof of concept for the others. Directly representative democracy offers many opportunities for theorizing about institutional reform beyond the deliberative town halls (at the federal level in the United States) that we propose here.

Critics argue that deliberative aspirations such as ours are hopelessly naive about the scale and complexity of modern politics. Average citizens cannot quit their day jobs to attend deliberative forums on all of the issues of the day. Indeed, professional politicians do not even have time to consider all such issues carefully. If anything, the political system needs ways to disburden people, not more ways to pull them into politics. Further, deliberative interactions can favor those with the most resources and the highest social status, and so can inadvertently reinforce inequalities in society.[10] Finally one might worry that elected officials themselves have few incentives to engage in deliberation and to incorporate deliberative interactions into their normal workflow. Deliberative democrats counter, however, that well-designed institutions can create opportunities for citizens and public officials alike to engage each other in substantive, constructive conversations that both will come to value.

CHANGE FOR THE BETTER?

Thus, we need to show not just that directly democratic reforms produce substantial change, but also that any differences are a change for the better. We will assess the quality of directly representative institutions by the five (mutually interactive) criteria that we previewed above:[11]

First, *inclusion: The institution should provide equal access and voice to and attract a wide cross-section of constituents,* expanding beyond those who are already influential under interest-group pluralism and

---

[10] Lynn M. Sanders, "Against Deliberation," *Political Theory* 25, no. 3 (1997): 347–76.

[11] These criteria vary in the extent to which institutional design can realize the desired outcome. For example, it will be much easier to guarantee a diverse audience through a well-designed recruitment strategy than encouraging trust and perceptions of legitimacy via design mechanisms. That said, good institutional design will attend to all the criteria insofar as possible.

standard partisan contestation.[12] A perfectly representative deliberative town hall is unattainable, if for no other reason than one cannot rightly compel people to participate. But a well-designed recruitment strategy can encourage a wide cross-section of the community to attend and participate. At the very least we would want to include voices that are less represented in standard interest-group pluralism and partisan politics. The institution should be more representative than standard participation profiles. Chapter 3 applies this criterion of access and representativeness to our deliberative town halls.

Second, *informed justification: The institution should encourage constituents to proceed on the basis of reliable, balanced, and relevant information, and cultivate a willingness to participate in the discussion effectively and constructively.* For a deliberative exchange to be of high quality, the parties to the exchange must feel (and actually be) empowered to participate meaningfully. Participants who are informed about the policy are more likely both to influence their representatives in consultation and to sensibly assess them as they exercise accountability.[13] Chapter 4 applies this criterion of information and capacity to our deliberative town halls.

Third, *good reason-giving: The institutional design should promote high quality exchanges between elected officials and their constituents.* One hallmark of quality discussion is people's willingness to consider the merits of policy proposals that do not match their initial predispositions. Because in-person town halls tend to attract strong supporters and opponents, often disintegrating into shouting matches, the representatives who call these meetings often want to script and control the discussion, and to stay on message as opposed to allowing for a free-flowing exchange. Civility and policy substance are not only typically good in themselves, they also facilitate meaningful participation by those who are turned off by what they perceive to be a rigged and irrational form of power politics.[14] Chapter 5 applies this criterion of reasoned interaction to our deliberative town halls.

---

[12] Of course, there should be room for members of Congress to meet with homogenous groups. We advance directly representative democracy as a supplement to such existing processes, not as a replacement.

[13] Scott L. Althaus, *Collective Preferences in Democratic Politics: Opinion Surveys and the Will of the People* (Cambridge: Cambridge University Press, 2003).

[14] As we note in the conclusion, there is an important relationship between some kinds of protest and deliberation.

Fourth, *promoting legitimacy*: *The process should encourage the trust and legitimacy that can sustain the deliberative process when participants are not able to reconvene.* As we have noted, we do not expect citizens to quit their day jobs. Representative democracy requires elected officials who can learn about policies and exercise their best judgment. But we *do* seek to shore up eroding perceptions of trust and deliberative legitimacy within the current representative system. Good deliberative events will generate warranted perceptions of legitimacy among citizens as well as provide elected officials the incentives actually to be trustworthy when they deliberate with their fellow legislators. Chapter 6 applies this criterion of trust and legitimacy to our deliberative town halls.

Fifth and finally, *scalability*: *The institution should be scalable so that a meaningful number of constituents can participate, and the process can perceptibly ramify through the larger deliberative system.* A representative institution that can only accommodate a very small number of constituents makes it difficult for those who cannot access the forums to engage in effective deliberative accountability. Moreover, very small-scale consultation is unlikely to influence patterns of deliberative exchange in the larger polity. Well-designed institutions should be able to operate on a meaningful scale. Chapter 7 applies this criterion of scale to our deliberative town halls.

Although this list does not exhaust all possible criteria, it does capture core features common to most notions of deliberative democratic legitimacy. If institutions meet a basic threshold on each criterion, the combination would greatly improve democratic quality.

THE STATE OF DIRECT REPRESENTATION

Why should we concern ourselves with designing new institutions to enhance representative-constituent communication now? Many opportunities for direct interaction already exist. Members of Congress meet with their constituents in both their Washington and district offices, reply to constituent mail, and send out newsletters, and maintain websites and social media accounts. Many of these traditional forms of interaction, however, do not reliably promote the standards that we outlined above. For example, we know from extensive news reporting that when representatives host town halls, these meetings often descend into shouting matches.[15] Sending newsletters, distributing press releases to the mass

---

[15] Jeff Zeleny, "Democrats Skip Town Halls to Avoid Voter Rage," *New York Times*, June 6, 2010, Accessed May 28, 2018. www.nytimes.com/2010/06/07/us/politics/07townhall

media, and answering constituent mail may help to advertise the representative's policy positions and activities, but they do not foster the two-way communication that connects citizens to government.[16]

The kinds of meetings that representatives now have with the public, which in the United States have come to be called "town halls," rarely meet our five criteria for effective deliberative institutions. First, the participants who make the effort to attend a town hall are not usually representative of the member's constituents. Instead, those who show up are often the representatives' strongest supporters or fiercest opponents, often also partisan and policy extremists, and often not persuadable by new facts or good arguments.[17] These town halls frequently fail to represent important sub-constituencies altogether.

In addition, the current town halls rarely provide balanced and credible information to help improve constituents' capacity to participate meaningfully in the discussion. Although standard town halls do allow participants to voice an opinion, the organizers typically make little effort to provide balanced policy information that would empower and enable participants to voice an informed opinion in the session.[18] Third, nondeliberative town halls tend to reinforce and entrench preexisting opinions. Even when they do not degenerate into shouting matches, few citizens leave the event having changed their minds. Fourth and finally, in-person town halls have inherent space and funding constraints. They cannot accommodate large numbers of constituents. At the same time, they impose relatively high costs to potential participants, who have to get to and from the event, hire a babysitter, and so on.

.html; and Heidi M. Przybyla, "Republicans avoid town halls after health care votes," *USA Today*, April 11, 2017, Accessed May 28, 2018. www.usatoday.com/story/news/politics/2017/04/10/republicans-avoid-town-halls-after-health-care-votes/100286290/. News reports suffer from selection, but as we show below, *none* of our sessions exhibited such problems.

[16] See David Lazer, Michael Neblo, and Kevin Esterling, "The Internet and the Madisonian Cycle: Possibilities and Prospects for Consultative Representation," in *Connecting Democracy: Online Consultation and the Flow of Political Communication*, ed. Stephen Coleman and Peter Shane (Cambridge, MA: MIT Press, 2011), 265–85. In the conclusion we discuss how some of these forms might be improved.

[17] Zeleny, "Democrats Skip Town Halls to Avoid Voter Rage." We note, though, that this representative made this claim while emphasizing that he has decided to keep doing face to face meetings, saying that he is "old-fashioned."

[18] We note that some third parties offer materials for effective participation in townhalls. See, for example: "9 Tips for Town Hall Meetings," NCOA, August 11, 2017, Accessed May 28, 2018. www.ncoa.org/public-policy-action/advocacy-toolkit/meeting-with-congress/town-hall-tips/. But the point is that one would want to pair the materials with the invitation in a more specific way.

Thus, even when a representative may institute consultative exchanges with constituents through in-person town halls, the representatives and citizens alike may rightly view such institutions as highly limited. Probably for these reasons, members of Congress seem recently to have scaled back face-to-face town halls considerably.[19]

THE PROMISE AND PERILS OF TECHNOLOGY

Today the Internet allows us to renegotiate the relationship between representatives and constituents, creating new opportunities to design directly representative institutions. The Internet offers democracy at the speed of light, seemingly unencumbered by the tax on communication that distance has levied for most of human existence.[20] It has enabled social movements around the world to coordinate rapidly, candidates to raise large amounts of "small money" in US politics, and politicians to bypass the mass media and speak directly to targeted groups and the larger public.[21] The interactive capacities of communication technology enable us to envision a new kind of town hall that is accessible and attractive to a broad cross-section of the population.

However, research on the potential of technology to improve the quality of democracy is often less sanguine.[22] Idealistic arguments from the early days of the web, that Internet-based technologies were intrinsically democratizing,[23] yielded to more pessimistic views suggesting that the Internet offered "politics as usual,"[24] or even dystopia. The logic of modern technology tends toward the like-minded sorting together and toward algorithms matching people with information that confirms their

---

[19] See, for example, Przybyla, "Republicans avoid town halls after health care votes."

[20] For an early statement regarding the prospects of technology to enable and facilitate interactive town halls in modern society, see Amitai Etzioni, "Minerva: An Electronic Town Hall," *Policy Sciences* 3, no. 4 (1972): 457–74; and Amitai Etzioni, Kenneth Laudon, and Sara Lipson, "Participatory Technology: The MINERVA Communications Tree," *The Journal of Communication* 25, no. 2 (June 1, 1975): 64–74.

[21] Beth Simone Noveck, *Smart Citizens, Smarter State: The Technologies of Expertise and the Future of Governing* (Cambridge, MA: Harvard University Press, 2015); and Stephen Coleman and Peter M. Shane, *Connecting Democracy: Online Consultation and the Flow of Political Communication* (Cambridge, MA: MIT Press, 2011).

[22] Andrew Chadwick, "Web 2.0: New Challenges for the Study of E-Democracy in an Era of Informational Exuberance," *ISJLP* 5 (2008): 9.

[23] Howard Rheingold, *The Virtual Community: Finding Connection in a Computerized World* (Boston: Addison-Wesley Longman Publishing Co., Inc., 1993).

[24] Scott Wright, "Politics as Usual? Revolution, Normalization and a New Agenda for Online Deliberation," *New Media & Society* 14, no. 2 (August 5, 2011): 244–61.

prior beliefs.[25] Social media seems a limited fix. Although 67 percent of adults report getting some news from social media,[26] they rarely discuss controversial matters via social media relative to face-to-face settings.[27] In nondemocratic countries the state uses the Internet to filter and manipulate the information to which people are exposed.[28] In countries such as China and Russia, many argue that the Internet has served as a powerful bulwark for an undemocratic order. Yet the "revolutionary potential" of the Internet lies in how it can be designed and used in particular contexts.[29]

The specific innovation we propose seeks to reenergize neglected practices of direct representation. The Internet offers tools to rewire the communication flows undergirding our democracy. The way citizens have adopted current interactive communications technologies creates more opportunities to participate in, learn about, criticize, and develop warranted trust in their government. Such technologies allow citizens a new kind of access, irrespective of their geographic proximity to the seat of government and increasingly irrespective of their wealth and educational level.

Chapter 2 lays out how interactive communication technology can create online what we call "deliberative town halls." The key ingredient of these town halls is simple: representatives regularly invite their constituents, from the comfort of their own living room or their public library, to converse substantively with them about key issues of the day. If embraced by members of Congress, our application would stand as a genuinely new institution of democratic representation. It would make possible more directly representative democracy.

A well-designed Internet strategy by members of Congress could provide citizens with information useful for understanding a policy as it develops and allow those citizens to interact more symmetrically with

---

[25] Cass R. Sunstein, *Republic.com 2.0* (Princeton, NJ: Princeton University Press, 2008); Eli Pariser, *The Filter Bubble: How the New Personalized Web Is Changing What We Read and How We Think* (London: Penguin, 2011).

[26] Jeffrey Gottfried and Elisa Shearer, "News Use across Social Media Platforms 2016," Pew Research Center, 2016.

[27] Keith N. Hampton et al., "Social Media and the 'Spiral of Silence'," *Pew Research Internet Project*, 2014.

[28] Gary King, Jennifer Pan, and Margaret E. Roberts, "How the Chinese Government Fabricates Social Media Posts for Strategic Distraction, Not Engaged Argument," *American Political Science Review* 111, no. 3 (August 2017): 484–501.

[29] Wright, "Politics as Usual? Revolution, Normalization and a New Agenda for Online Deliberation," 246.

both their member of Congress and with each other. Wisely used, the Internet can reconnect citizens and Congress.

As we will demonstrate, deliberative town halls based on Internet technology can, to a great degree, satisfy the five criteria for a well-designed representative institution. Online deliberative town halls offer widespread, easy access to consultations given the increasing penetration of the internet. The technology enables citizens to become informed given the low cost of finding relevant information on the Internet. Web technology is interactive and so can foster discursive exchanges among citizens as well as between citizens and their representative. This basis in information and good deliberation generates trust. And the process can easily scale up from small to large groups.

Currently Congress makes very limited use of deliberative town halls.[30] Making effective use of innovations requires new knowledge and new operating procedures among officeholders, and adopting new technology always involves unknown risks. Members of Congress may reasonably be reluctant to embrace new technology.

First, while online technology reduces the costs for constituents from all walks of life to gain access, members of Congress might not always want to seek out a diverse audience. Instead they might prefer microtargeting – customizing their message to very narrow constituencies – speaking directly with their strong supporters, or even exchanging expressive arguments with opponents, rather than engaging with a town hall of diverse constituents. For their part, constituents also tend to seek out discussion among those who already agree with them, or, for some, seek out opportunities for partisan combat. Both representatives and constituents may have incentives to exploit the Internet's tools to sort and filter their participation into echo chambers or to shout down those with whom they disagree.[31]

In addition, although the Internet does reduce the cost of finding information, representatives might reasonably be concerned about the

---

[30] Chadwick, "Web 2.0: New Challenges for the Study of E-Democracy in an Era of Informational Exuberance"; Kevin M. Esterling, David M.J. Lazer, and Michael A. Neblo, "Improving Congressional Websites," (Center for Technology Innovation at Brookings, 2010); and Collin Burden et al., "2007 Gold Mouse Report: Lessons from the Best Web Sites on Capitol Hill," (Congressional Management Foundation, 2007).

[31] Cass R. Sunstein, *#Republic: Divided Democracy in the Age of Social Media* (Princeton, NJ: Princeton University Press, 2017); Pariser, *The Filter Bubble: How the New Personalized Web Is Changing What We Read and How We Think*; and Bakshy, Messing, and Adamic, "Exposure to Ideologically Diverse News and Opinion on Facebook," *Science* 348, no. 6239 (June 5, 2015): 1130–2.

quality of information that constituents can find online. While constituents may easily find content and information that speaks to their policy concerns, such information is often unbalanced and sometimes based on falsehood.[32]

Although the technology of deliberative town halls is interactive and allows for direct and reciprocal communication between the representative and constituents, officials may rightly have concerns about the civility of online forums. In many online contexts, poorly designed institutions deepen partisan rigidity and polarization. Hiding behind anonymous screen names, participants evade the normal constraints on incivility.[33]

Without typically having technical backgrounds, members of Congress may not know how to evaluate the prospects for harnessing the interactivity and scalability of Web-based applications. Even if they could solve the technical hurdles to implement deliberative town halls, they might suspect that the online mobilization of citizens would be superficial, a variant of hashtag activism, or highly dependent on interested parties from outside the district.

Finally, legislators are often wary of adopting new technology due to their common concerns about reelection. Some may fear losing control of their message when they open up their official communication to interactive exchanges. Others might worry that participants will engage in uncivil discourse when commenting in online forums, and so create a permanent record, available to future searches or viral social media propagation, that might seemingly connect their office to uncivil, vitriolic, or offensive language.[34]

Thus, while interactive online communication technology creates opportunities to develop new institutions that at least have the potential to meet our five criteria, it is perhaps no surprise that representatives have not rushed to embrace technological change. The quality and technical capabilities of congressional websites have lagged behind those of commercial websites. Members of Congress have found that adopting

[32] D. J. Flynn, Brendan Nyhan, and Jason Reifler, "The Nature and Origins of Misperceptions: Understanding False and Unsupported Beliefs About Politics," *Political Psychology* 38, no. S1 (February 1, 2017): 127–50; and Adam J. Berinsky, "Rumors and Health Care Reform: Experiments in Political Misinformation," *British Journal of Political Science* (2015): 1–22.

[33] Gina Masullo Chen, *Online Incivility and Public Debate: Nasty Talk* (New York: Palgrave Macmillan, 2017).

[34] Lazer, Neblo, and Esterling, "The Internet and the Madisonian Cycle: Possibilities and Prospects for Consultative Representation."

interactive communication technologies is neither automatic nor effort-less.[35] Would-be democratic reformers need to understand incentives and resistance to new technology in order to propose effective and adaptable solutions. Legislators need evidence that the new technology is actually beneficial to both them and their constituents.

CONCLUSION

Representative democracy appears to be trapped in a bad equilibrium: neither citizens nor representatives actively demand enhanced consulta-tive democracy unprompted, despite preferring it under an expanded set of choices, as we will show. Since existing town halls tend to be limited in their capacity to promote high quality interactions between citizens and their elected officials, neither citizens nor representatives have good models to help them envision a consultative alternative that can incor-porate directly representative participation. Elected officials are reluc-tant to embrace new consultative institutions when those institutions are technology-driven.

Our task below is to assess the degree to which our online deliberative town halls measure up to our five criteria. Because we are proposing a new institution to enhance directly representative practices in modern democracy, the burden of proof lies with us to demonstrate that such an institution is both feasible and desirable.

The next chapter describes the institutional innovation of deliberative town halls. The remainder of the book demonstrates just how this institu-tion makes directly representative democracy more feasible just as it has become more needed.

---

[35] Kevin M. Esterling, David M. J. Lazer, and Michael A. Neblo, "Representative Communication: Web Site Interactivity and Distributional Path Dependence in the US Congress," *Political Communication* 28, no. 4 (2011): 409–39; Jane E. Fountain, *Building the Virtual State: Information Technology and Institutional Change* (Washington, DC: Brookings Institution Press, 2001); Kevin M. Esterling, David M. J. Lazer, and Michael A. Neblo, "Connecting to Constituents," *Political Research Quarterly* 66, no. 1 (2012): 102–14; and David Lazer et al., "The Multiple Institutional Logics of Innovation," *International Public Management Journal* 14, no. 3 (2011): 311–40.

2

Building a New Home Style

> The more one observes members of Congress at work in their districts, the more impressed one is by the simple fact that people are hard to find. Members (and their staffs) expend incredible amounts of time and energy just trying to locate people to present themselves to ... But people, it turns out, do not arrange themselves for the convenience of their member of Congress.
>
> —Richard Fenno, *Home Style*

The great political scientist Richard Fenno spent his career observing members of Congress as they went about their daily business. In his celebrated book, *Home Style: House Members in Their Districts*,[1] he documents the enormous efforts that elected officials invest in reaching out to their constituents back home in their districts. Reading Fenno, one gets the distinct impression that members of Congress, themselves, want a more directly representative democracy (whether such a desire is based on political principle, electoral prudence, or both). But the numerical and geographic size of districts, the complexity of governance, and difficulty reaching representative groups of citizens in a mass democracy have until now combined to make direct representation a challenge. It is true that constituents "do not arrange themselves for the convenience of their member of Congress." With new communication technology, however, the members can now arrange themselves for the convenience of their constituents. Such arrangements make an enormous difference in who engages with their representatives and how.

---

[1] Fenno, *Home Style: House Members in Their Districts*.

We do not argue that representatives should abandon the usual channels of mass communication via parties and interest groups. No modern democracy can function without organizations that formally represent interests. We do argue, however, against the belief that the status quo, in which democratic participation amounts to little more than check writing, voting, and protesting, encompasses all of what we can hope to do as democratic citizens.

In this chapter we describe our experiments in democratic consultation. We use our online deliberative town hall platform to test our claims about the transformative potential of technology. These are not laboratory experiments with research subjects who temporarily adopt the roles of representatives and constituents. They involve actual members of Congress using a technology that all representatives could easily implement themselves. In these experiments we recruited a diverse group of members of the House of Representatives to conduct deliberative town halls, and invited representative samples of their constituents to participate in them, along with a control group that did not participate. The simple technology we used could be scaled up to make interactive, substantive discussions between citizens and their representatives felt in the larger political system. The members of Congress were enthusiastic about participating in our experiment and eager to explore the possibilities of the new technology.

DESIGN OF THE ONLINE TOWN HALL PLATFORM

In the summer of 2006, in collaboration with our partners at the Congressional Management Foundation (CMF),[2] we hosted a series of nineteen online deliberative town hall meetings to discuss immigration reform with members of the US House of Representatives from twelve congressional districts.[3]

---

[2] The evaluation of the online deliberative town halls was a collaboration between the authors and the Congressional Management Foundation (CMF, Accessed May 28, 2018. http://congressfoundation.org/). CMF recruited the representatives to participate, and were extensively involved in the design of the online platform as well as in the protocol and implementation for the sessions themselves. The project was funded by a grant from the Digital Government program of the National Science Foundation (IIS-0429452), and the Committee on House Administration of the U.S. House of Representatives was the collaborating government organization on the grant. Curt Ziniel, who was a graduate student at University of California, Riverside at the time, was our research assistant and did much of the staffing for the sessions themselves. We are very grateful for the efforts of all of these collaborators and the support from NSF.

[3] We also hosted a larger deliberative town hall meeting on terrorism policy using the same platform in collaboration with Senator Carl Levin (D-MI) in the summer of 2008. We

We chose immigration as the topic in consultation with the House members who participated in our study. The majority of members were interested in having the town halls focus on this topic because immigration was the most prominent domestic issue on the national agenda in the summer of 2006. When we initially pitched the idea of doing this study to members of Congress, our proposal was to focus on a relatively low-controversy topic – health savings accounts. All of the members responded that they wanted to tackle immigration precisely because it was controversial.

The issue of immigration has changed significantly since we ran our experiments, as has US politics more generally. The interval raises the question of whether we would observe similar results in today's political climate. Although it is impossible to say for sure, we have several reasons to believe we would see similar results. First, we have new projects with members of Congress in the field, and the members continue to be interested in leveraging communication technology to interact with their constituents. Second, even back in 2006, the two parties were already quite polarized (see Figure I.1 above). Most importantly, one of the most consistent findings from the entire deliberation literature is that well-structured deliberation tends to depolarize participants.[4] So it is plausible that, given increasing polarization, we would see even more dramatic results from deliberation today.

In Chapter 7, we replicate our findings on a completely different issue, detainee policy (e.g., torture, rendition, etc.). We thus have evidence that our results are not narrowly dependent on the issue of immigration. Yet we do not claim that directly representative practices would prove equally useful for all issues. We expect that they will work best when an issue combines both moral and technical dimensions to a high degree (e.g., health care), rather than those that are largely moral (e.g., abortion) or largely technical (e.g., building codes). But ultimately this is an empirical question. In our larger reform vision, we anticipate deliberative town hall sessions on a wide range of issues, chosen perhaps by a national commission akin to that for presidential debates. In this book, we restrict ourselves to a proof of concept, with a replication, on two important and controversial issues.

---

defer discussion of the session with Senator Levin to Chapter 7 since it differed from the House sessions in important ways that allow us to test the robustness and scalability of our innovations.

[4] Marina Lindell et al., "What drives the polarisation and moderation of opinions? Evidence from a Finnish citizen deliberation experiment on immigration," *European Journal of Political Research* 56.1 (2017): 23–45.

Each of our nineteen deliberative town halls began with a survey research company contacting a random sample of the constituents of a member of the US Congress who had agreed to work with us. About 35 percent of those contacted agreed to participate in a 35-minute session with other constituents and their member of Congress. Constituents were told ahead of time they would have an opportunity to pose their questions and comments to the member on the topic of immigration policy. To help constituents prepare for their session, we gave them background reading material on the topic of immigration policy based on nonpartisan reports produced by congressional research offices. (We reproduce the background reading material in Chapter 4.)

Once on their computer, the participants logged into the session to join other citizens and their member of Congress for the discussion. Figure 2.1 shows a screenshot of the platform from one of our sessions from the constituents' viewpoint. The user interface has four elements. On the left is a photograph of the representative who is hosting the discussion, in this case George Radanovich, a Republican who at the time represented California's 14th Congressional District. Moving counterclockwise, at the bottom is an open textbox that the constituents (in this case Debbie) used to type questions and comments, which, when submitted, were posted to a queue visible only to the study personnel.

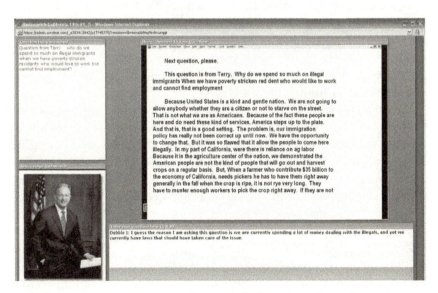

FIGURE 2.1. *Online town hall user interface*

Constituents were free to ask any questions and make any comments they chose, provided the questions and comments remained on topic. In the screenshot illustrated, a constituent named "Debbie" has typed in the comment, "I guess the reason I am asking this question is we are currently spending a lot of money dealing with the illegals, and yet we currently have laws that should have taken care of the issue." Once Debbie pressed enter, this comment appeared in the queue.

A member of the research team posted the incoming questions and comments to the textbox in the upper-left corner of the interface, one at a time, roughly in the order they arrived in the queue. The research team filtered questions for redundancy and germaneness, as well as to ensure that everyone in the discussion group had an opportunity to participate, but otherwise did not filter on the substance of the comments. At the time of this screenshot, the moderator had already posted a question from a constituent named "Terri" asking Congressman Radanovich "Why do we spend so much on illegal immigrants when we have poverty stricken residents who would love to work but cannot find employment?"

As questions and comments such as those from Debbie or Terri arrived into the session, the representative would first read the question out loud, and then address the question orally through a telephone connection using Voice over IP technology. Constituents could hear the representative's voice if they had speakers connected to their computers. In addition, a captionist transcribed the representative's statements in real time, and those transcribed statements scrolled through the textbox at the top-right of the platform. Including the real-time captioning ensured accessibility for the hearing-impaired, made it easier for people to process the information through reading as well as hearing, and reduced any issues that might result from audio problems.

The sessions were entirely unscripted – the representative knew that the topic would be immigration policy but did not know in advance what questions the constituents would ask. Typically, the representative hosting the event first read the question or comment aloud, and then responded in a conversational manner. The screenshot reflects this process in the real-time captioning box on the top-right, where Representative Radanovich first said, "Next question, please," then read out loud Terri's question about public spending on illegal immigrants, and then responded, "Because the United States is a kind and gentle nation. We are not going to allow anybody whether they are a citizen or not to starve on the street. This is not what we are as Americans…" He continued, in comments that do not appear in this screenshot, to recognize the immigration system is flawed and in need of repair, but that the policy needs to accommodate the needs of farmers in his central California district.

We developed this online platform using off-the-shelf software that was available in 2006. The interface did not include streaming video of the representative, both because broadband limits and graphics cards at the time did not reliably support streaming video, and because at that time few representatives had web cameras and microphones on their computers. Instead, we presented a still image of the representative, which in each case was the representative's official photograph. For similar reasons we did not build in voice or video for the constituents.

STRUCTURED COMMUNICATION IN THE ONLINE TOWN HALL

Directly representative democracy seeks to enhance deliberative communication between citizens and their government officials. But not all channels of communication qualify as either deliberative or directly representative. Neither "tweet storms" nor "astroturf" lobbying campaigns of mass emails from organized groups are likely to meet our five standards. To begin to meet these criteria the communication channel and the architecture of the communication platform should be structured to induce a constructive exchange between citizens and elected officials.

Our online deliberative town hall platform included several design elements that we expected would help promote deliberative discussion. First, we recruited a broad and representative group of participants to ensure that the diverse perspectives of each congressional district would be articulated. Second, we provided the town hall participants high quality, ideologically balanced background reading materials (approved by all thirteen offices), so that each participant could be empowered to contribute to the conversation in an informed, confident, and compelling way. Third, each session included a screener who helped avoid redundancy and ensured that as many people who wished to participate in the conversation could do so. Fourth, in each session a member of the research team served as a neutral moderator, signaling to participants that the session was hosted by an organization independent of the representative's office. Fifth, the sessions were fully unscripted, real-time interactions where the representative had to respond herself, without assistance of staff. Sixth, the technology enabled the representative to communicate her responses orally, both verifying to the constituents that the speaker was the representative, not a staffer or other person posing as the representative, and letting the constituents hear the representative's tone and demeanor. Finally, the communication technology greatly reduced costs of access for the participants. The online technology reduced interpersonal barriers to participating, facilitating participation by those who might be shy or conflict averse in face-to-face settings.

DESIGN OF THE EXPERIMENT

We evaluated our online deliberative town hall platform using a "randomized control trial" (RCT) experimental design, in which we randomly assigned some constituents to receive an invitation to the deliberative town hall (the deliberative "treatment" group), another group to receive information only (the "information-only" group), and a third group to take the surveys only (the "true control" group). With the RCT design, we can evaluate whether participation in the online town hall enhanced constituents' knowledge of policies, their attitudes toward policy options, their trust in and approval of the representative, and their feelings of political efficacy.

Such an evaluation plan is similar to how clinical researchers conduct a drug efficacy trial, where study participants are randomly assigned to treatment groups who receive the drug and control groups who do not. Although we used computers to do the randomization, it was no different than flipping a coin to determine whether constituents are invited to participate in a town hall. Randomization ensures no extraneous differences between those randomized to participate and not to participate. Thus, the only difference between the participants and the nonparticipants was exposure to a deliberative town hall session. The design allows us to identify the distinct *causal* effect of directly representative consultation on the constituents.[5]

---

[5] Using this RCT design was crucial in order to subject our platform to a rigorous evaluation. Randomizing the invitation to participate in this way enabled us to create scientifically meaningful comparison groups between those who experienced our new online deliberative town hall and those who did not. If instead we had allowed constituents to choose whether to be in the treatment or control group, instead of randomizing, that would create a problem for our evaluation since the constituents in each group would not be comparable to each other. For example, those who already had the highest level of policy knowledge might be the ones who select into the sessions, and so a straight comparison between those who participate in the sessions to those who do not would mistakenly attribute knowledge differences to participation in our platform, rather than to differences between the participants themselves.

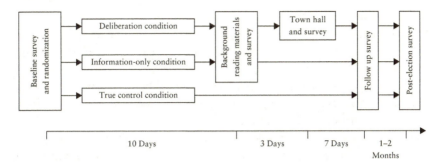

FIGURE 2.2. *The experimental design for the House of Representatives study*

Figure 2.2 depicts the flow of the study. Participants who complied with all aspects of the study followed one of the horizontal paths indicated by a solid arrow. Participants, however, were free not to comply with their assignment in the study design. As we describe in more detail below, some constituents deviated from their intended paths. (In the appendix we describe our analytical strategies for reconstructing scientifically meaningful comparison groups under these circumstances.[6])

Knowledge Networks (KN), an online polling firm, recruited a sample of constituents from each representative's congressional district. For each session, we recruited over one hundred voting-age constituents to be assigned to our treatment and control conditions. We chose to work with KN because they take great pains to recruit a representative sample of participants, providing free Internet access to those who did not have those services already. Using KN helped to recruit a broad and fairly representative cross section of constituents from each of the congressional districts. In Chapter 3, we describe in detail the citizens who participated in our study.

As a first step, we administered a baseline survey using KN's online survey platform. The baseline survey was extensive and measured constituents' attitudes regarding government and their representative, their immigration policy knowledge and preferences, and individual traits such as conflict aversion and feelings of political efficacy.

After each group completed their baseline surveys, we asked the respondents whether they were willing and able to participate in an online deliberative town hall with their representative of Congress, giving

---

[6] The technical version of the methods we use can be found in our article, Kevin M. Esterling, Michael A. Neblo, and David M. J. Lazer, "Estimating Treatment Effects in the Presence of Noncompliance and Nonresponse: The Generalized Endogenous Treatment Model," *Political Analysis* 19, no. 2 (Spring 2011): 205–26.

the date and time of the upcoming sessions for their congressional district. Among those who indicated they were both willing and able to participate at the given time, we randomized the constituents to one of three experimental groups shown in Figure 2.2: A *deliberation group* condition (DG) where constituents were invited to the deliberative town hall, or to one of our two comparison groups, an *information-only* condition (IO), and a *true control* condition (TC).

Constituents that were randomly assigned to the deliberative group condition (DG) were given an invitation to participate in an upcoming online deliberative town hall with their representative. We provided reading material on immigration policy electronically both to the information-only participants and to the deliberative group participants, after they received their invitation but before their session occurred. The reading material gave constituents an opportunity to learn about the policy, first so that each participant felt empowered to participate actively in the discussion, and second, to facilitate a more informed and productive town hall. The background reading, of about three single spaced pages, provided factual information relevant to immigration policy, developed by summarizing and editing for brevity and reading level nonpartisan policy briefs written by the Congressional Budget Office.[7] In order to prevent the reading material from influencing the course of the discussions, we went to some length to use language that was objective and politically unbiased. The participating representatives, both Republicans and Democrats, all vetted and signed off on the briefing materials, which we reproduce and discuss in Chapter 4. Each member of Congress participated in the session for thirty-five minutes. At the conclusion of the session, the member and any Congressional staff logged off the platform and the constituents were given twenty-five additional minutes to discuss the session with each other via a text-based chat room.

The constituents assigned to the information only (IO) condition were provided the reading material and filled out surveys, but were not invited to attend the deliberative town hall itself (in order to rule out the possibility that any changes from participating in the deliberative town hall resulted merely from learning more information). Constituents assigned to the true control (TC) condition received neither the reading material

---

[7] Caldera Selena and Paige Piper/Bach, "Immigration Policy in the United States," *Congressional Budget Office*, February 2006, Accessed May 28, 2018. //www.cbo.gov/publication /17625; and Nabeel Alsalam, "Role of Immigrants in the U.S. Labor Market: An Update," Washington, DC: Congressional Budget Office, 2010, Accessed May 28, 2018. www.cbo .gov/sites/default/fles/cbofles/ftpdocs/116xx/doc11691/07–23 immigrants_in_labor_force .pdf.

nor an invitation to attend the deliberative town hall; they just filled out surveys. We compare these two control groups (IO and TC) to the deliberative town hall participants (DG) to evaluate the causal effects of exposure to the deliberative town hall.

About seven days following each deliberative town hall event, we asked constituents across all three conditions to fill out a follow up survey that largely mirrored the baseline survey. This follow up survey measured the outcomes we used for our evaluation and that we focus on for the remainder of the book. These included the constituents' knowledge of immigration policy, their preferences on immigration policy, and their attitudes toward the representative and the deliberative town hall sessions themselves. We also administered a short survey to the constituents from all three groups about four months later, immediately following the November 2006 mid-term elections. We draw on this survey for the evaluation as well, including whether participating in the deliberative town hall session made the constituents more likely to vote.

WHICH MEMBERS OF CONGRESS PARTICIPATED?

The Congressional Management Foundation (CMF), a nonpartisan, nonprofit organization dedicated to advising congressional offices in management practices, helped to recruit the participating members of Congress. We worked hard to balance the representatives across regional and party lines, as well as other criteria. Table 2.1 lists the members of the House of Representatives who hosted one or more online deliberative town hall events for our study. They were broadly reflective of the House as a whole. They were all running for reelection: five were Republicans, seven Democrats, and the districts were drawn from each region of the country. Representatives Capuano, Conaway, Eshoo, Kingston, Price, Radanovich and Weldon each hosted two events, and Representatives Blumenauer, Clyburn, Lofgren, Manzullo and Matheson each hosted one. There were two women (Eshoo and Lofgren), one African-American member (Clyburn), one member from each party's leadership (Kingston and Clyburn), and one member from each party who differed with their party on the issue of immigration policy (Radanovich and Matheson).

The first four columns of Table 2.1 demonstrate that the representatives who participated in our research project were diverse in terms of party, geography, time in office, and most recent margin of victory. Figure 2.3 shows a map of the party and geographic distribution of the

TABLE 2.1. *Participating members of Congress*

Member	Party	District	Term	Percent of vote 2004	Ideology score
Earl Blumenauer	D	OR-3	6	71	−0.478
Michael Capuano	D	MA-8	4	Uncontested	−0.598
James Clyburn	D	SC-6	7	67	−0.450
Mike Conaway	R	TX-11	1	77	+0.571
Anna Eshoo	D	CA-14	7	63	−0.427
Jack Kingston	R	GA-1	7	Uncontested	+0.514
Zoe Lofgren	D	CA-16	6	71	−0.447
Don Manzullo	R	IL-16	7	69	+0.514
Jim Matheson	D	UT-2	3	56	−.0119
David Price	D	NC-4	9	64	−0.307
George Radanovich	R	CA-19	6	66	+0.503
Dave Weldon	R	FL-15	6	65	0.479

Senator Carl Levin (D-Michigan) also conducted a session that we describe in Chapter 7.

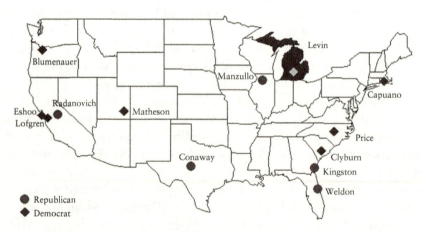

FIGURE 2.3. *Members and districts in the study, 2006 and 2008*

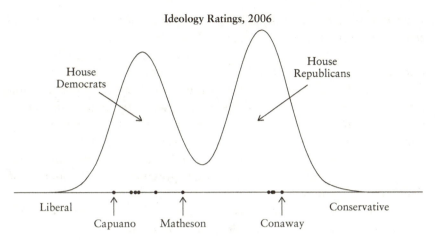

FIGURE 2.4. *Ideology ratings for participating members, 2006*

representatives and their districts. (Senator Carl Levin, D-MI, also conducted a session with 175 of his constituents during the summer of 2008 in which he discussed terrorist detainee policy. In Chapter 7, we describe Sen. Levin's session separately and in detail.)

The fifth column of Table 2.1 reports representatives' political ideology using a standard measure of legislators' location on a liberal-conservative (left-right) ideology scale.[8] The curve in Figure 2.4 shows the distribution of ideology scores for the whole House of Representatives (the farther to the left, the more liberal the score) as well as dots indicating the scores for the individual representatives who participated in our study. In general, the Republican representatives were within the middle range of House Republicans, and likewise the Democrats were generally in the middle of the House Democrats, with the exception of Representative Matheson, a conservative Democrat. Representative Capuano was the most liberal Democrat and Representative Conaway the most conservative Republican in our study.

This group was also about typical in technology use. For example, we examined the score for each member's "Gold Mouse" award rating, assigned by CMF for the quality of their official website. CMF rated the quality of each member's website along a variety of criteria and created an index to summarize each website's overall quality score that ranges

[8] The measure is known as the DW-NOMINATE scale. See www.voteview.com (Accessed May 28, 2018).

from zero to one hundred. One can take the score as a measure of the relative priority the representative places on website and electronic communication with constituents. And while most of the scores among our members are above the chamber median of fifty, there is variation here too, with five scores at or below the median; we were not working merely with the technophiles in the House. We tested many other commonly used metrics and typologies for members of Congress as well, and discerned no striking features that set our group apart. For example, our group's legislative effectiveness scores (used to measure legislators' ability to advance legislation through Congress) closely mirrors that of the House as a whole.[9]

Since these representatives selected themselves into the study, we should be attentive to whether our results generalize to the rest of Congress.[10] Beyond the mere fact of participating, we do not have any strong reasons to believe that our group of representatives is all that unusual compared to their colleagues. In particular, all members of Congress have an incentive to find low cost ways to communicate with their constituents. And the risks for representatives to participate were very low in that the project had the endorsement of the Congressional Management Foundation and the approval of the Committee on House Administration.

Even if it is true, however, that online communication only works well for the kinds of representatives who selected into our study, that success is likely to be felt at higher rates among future representatives who choose to engage in online communication. That is, this self-selection would work in favor of reinforcing enhanced democratic representation if it is the case that representatives who choose not to engage in online consultation are the ones who are particularly bad at it, and the ones who chose to engage in online consultation are those who are good at it. While we cannot decisively resolve this question with our current study, we hope to have shown that our results are likely to generalize to a broad swath of current and future representatives.

---

[9] For a comprehensive listing of legislative effectiveness scores for members of Congress, see Craig Volden and Alan E. Wiseman, *Legislative Effectiveness in the United States Congress: The Lawmakers* (New York: Cambridge University Press, 2014); or the book's website: www.thelawmakers.org (Accessed May 28, 2018).

[10] Much of the knowledge political scientists have of representatives' behavior comes from studies of representatives who were willing to grant unusual access to political scientists. For example, the discipline has long taken Fenno's *Home Style* as a reliable source of insights into district-based representation, and the representatives in his study were the type that let a political scientist follow them around to constituent events.

REPRESENTATIVES' VIEWS OF THE PLATFORM

The representatives who participated in the study were very positive about testing our platform, even knowing that it was experimental. The opening remarks that they made at the beginning of the sessions are useful for illustrating their positive attitude toward the platform and the experiment. For example, Rep. Earl Blumenauer states in his opening comment:

Let me begin by saying that I'm pleased to be a part of this experiment about ways to better communicate with government constituents on the issues of the day. One of the hardest parts of this job is being two places at once, separated usually by three time zones ... So I look forward to this evening's visit. I look forward to answering questions, hearing observations, and exploring the ways that we can better utilize technology to improve these links between citizens and their government.

Likewise, Congresswoman Lofgren stated,

It's good to be part of this experiment with the Congressional Management Foundation and to see how this works for my constituents and getting feedback. As most of my constituents know I come back home to San Jose virtually every week and I get a lot of opportunity for face to face contact, but obviously there's hundreds, thousands of people in the 16th district and I don't see all of them every time I come back, so this may be a way to expand methods to get information. I get a lot of e-mails from constituents, but hopefully this will be a new way to communicate.

And Congressman Conaway,

Thank you for joining us this afternoon on this opportunity to use technology to share some information, maybe some of the information of my views and maybe give me some information regarding your views on a really tough subject of immigration and border security that is in the news obviously every single day and is a topic of each of the town hall meetings and group gatherings that I have conducted throughout the district.

In each case, the representative is clearly self-conscious about participating in an experiment, and enthusiastic about testing out new technology to find best practices for enhancing representative-constituent interaction.

CONCLUSION

We bear the burden of proof to show whether our sessions met the five criteria for an effective directly representative event. But the design of our experiment ensures that we can evaluate the sessions rigorously. In the remainder of the book, we evaluate whether the directly representative encounters, *in practice*, met the five criteria that we set out in Chapter 1. Specifically, using this new online platform we evaluate: whether a wide cross section of constituents wanted to and did participate (Chapter 3); whether constituents developed the personal and informational capacity to participate effectively (Chapter 4); whether they were engaged in and open to being influenced by a high quality process (Chapter 5); whether they believed that the sessions reflected their conception of represent-ative democracy, enjoyed the experience and would do future sessions (Chapter 6); and finally (Chapter 7), whether the technology can scale up and out to include a critical mass of constituents. Each empirical chapter argues against a set of skeptics who dismiss the prospects for directly representative democracy, in light of their understanding of how a mass democracy can work.

Taken together, the results demonstrate the promise for directly repre-sentative democracy to augment participation beyond voting, donating, or protesting – that is, to reconnect constituents' voices to representative government.

3

Half of Democracy

You can't create crowds. So you go where people meet. That means you spend more time talking to groups like the Chamber of Commerce than you do to people who live along the road here ... The great mass of people you can't reach. They are not organized. They don't have institutions that you can plug into. The leadership, the elite, runs along the top of all the institutions, and you can reach them, but not the people generally.

—A member of Congress[1]

"Half of democracy" Ralph Nader once quipped, "is just showing up." By that measure most people do not even half-engage their democracy, because they do not show up for much. Barely half of eligible voters show up for US presidential races, and the numbers go down from there for other forms of political participation. Why? The member of Congress quoted above offers one prominent explanation: most citizens are not organized and have few institutional points of contact with the political system. It should come as no surprise, then, that politics would revolve almost exclusively around elites and interest groups since they are the only ones who can be reached. This arrangement generates cynicism and further disengagement on the part of "people who live along the road." But a more directly representative system would seem to be practically impossible, since its whole point is to bypass organized groups to reach nonelite citizens *as* citizens. Thus, our first criterion for improving democracy, promoting an equal voice for a wide cross section of citizens, would seem to be a pipe dream.

---

[1] Quoted anonymously in Fenno, *Home Style: House Members in Their Districts*, 235.

But imagine if members of Congress *could* engage the people along the road. What if the great mass of people had a routine way to interact with and engage legislators that was easily accessible? As we have argued, communication technology has radically altered elected officials' ability to reach out to their constituents *as* citizens rather than as members of parties and interest groups. Moreover, six out of seven citizens who have never attended a meeting to discuss public affairs reported that they had never been invited to do so.[2] If access and outreach really are at the root of low participation, then improvements in republican consultation and deliberative accountability are genuinely possible with better communicative infrastructure.

Perhaps, however, there is a more basic explanation for the lack of political participation. People may simply not *want* to participate, either because they are apathetic, they are content to free-ride, they hate politics, or they just have better things to do. If so, then there is little reason to suppose that institutional innovations in direct representation will actually engage a much broader swath of the public.[3]

Skeptics might reasonably worry that our reforms would be a waste of resources on precisely these grounds. If large portions of the public do not even turn out to vote, why should we think that they will show any capacity or desire to engage in time-consuming and detailed discussion of policy? On this view, most Americans want nothing to do with a more directly representative democracy, and cajoling them into more consultative participation would be paternalistic and counterproductive.

Our central claim, however, is that much of today's nonparticipation among our fellow citizens is rooted in disaffection with the options they have available to them (or, more to the point, don't have available to them) to participate constructively within status quo politics. Contemporary mass democracy mostly asks citizens to write checks, cast votes, and perhaps attend a protest. These tasks have little to do with reasoning about policy. We conjecture that current patterns of engagement do not reflect

---

[2] See Lawrence R. Jacobs, Fay Lomax Cook, and Michael X. Delli Carpini, *Talking Together: Public Deliberation and Political Participation in America* (Chicago: University of Chicago Press, 2009).

[3] On the relationship between normative and empirical analyses see Michael A. Neblo, "Philosophical Psychology with Political Intent," in *The Affect Effect*, eds. W. Russell Neuman, George E. Marcus, Michael MacKuen, and Ann N. Crigler (Chicago: University of Chicago Press, 2007), 25–47; Michael A. Neblo et al., "The Need for a Translational Science of Democracy," *Science* 355, no. 6328 (March 3, 2017): 914–15; and Michael Neblo, "Giving Hands and Feet to Morality," *Perspectives on Politics* 2, no. 1 (2004): 99–100.

how citizens would participate *if they were invited and given more attractive opportunities to do so*. While citizens might be demobilized by what they see as a corrupt interest-group system and bitterly partisan politics, that does not mean that they would lack enthusiasm for participating in a more directly representative system.[4]

In this chapter, we first test our claim about the source of nonparticipation directly, and find much stronger evidence that it is frustration rather than apathy that alienates people from politics. This finding sets the stage for new directly representative opportunities as a plausible supplement to the status quo. Using a large, national sample, we then analyze the determinants of people's *hypothetical* willingness to participate in new forums. However, some citizens may wish to appear more civically oriented than they really are, and answering a survey question might be merely "cheap talk." Thus, we also analyze the determinants of people's *actual* participation in response to the invitations to our online deliberative town hall forums. We find that willingness to participate in directly representative town halls is much more widespread than expected; that it is precisely people who are less likely to participate in traditional politics who are most interested in new forms of participation; and that people are attracted to such participation as an alternative to "politics as usual." Average citizens clearly do not regard directly representative opportunities as filigree on "real" politics or as an indulgence for political activists and intellectuals.

DELIBERATION'S SKEPTICS

Many writers have noted people's reluctance to participate in politics, and they point to two powerful reasons. First, citizens may choose not to participate out of a belief that they cannot make a difference. This belief can deter all forms of participation, including voting, protesting, campaigning, contributing, or deliberating. One way to understand this reluctance to participate is that citizens face a "collective action" problem, in that all citizens have a vested interest in the laws and public policies that the government creates, but since no one individual can control policy decisions, each citizen has little reason to invest the time and effort to participate. Those who do "show up" are those who find it easiest to

---

4 This chapter is largely based on our article Neblo et al., "Who Wants To Deliberate—And Why?" Ryan Kennedy and Anand Sokhey were our coauthors on the journal article and we gratefully acknowledge their contributions.

bear the costs of participating, such as the wealthy and well educated, and the most ideologically extreme. The citizens who do not show up are willing to "free ride" on the efforts of others who do pay attention to politics and participate.

Second, even if citizens were to overcome the collective action problem, many scholars note that citizens often find the conflict and disagreement inherent to democratic politics distasteful. For example, scholars claim that many citizens avoid politics out of an aversion to conflict, and go to great lengths to avoid exposing themselves to differing ideas and viewpoints. They may also worry about disapproval from others.[5] So, while the collective action problem applies to all forms of political participation, conflict aversion applies with special force to the kinds of deliberative town halls that directly representative democrats hope to foster.

On this view, adding opportunities for citizens to deliberate is badly misguided. On the one hand, most citizens would be unlikely even to show up, and those who do show up would then be unlikely to be representative of the larger population. Indeed, if those who show up tend to come from the upper classes in society, then deliberation would perversely and perhaps unintentionally magnify disparities that arise from current inequalities. Moreover, inducing citizens to participate would run counter to their own instincts and preferences, creating resentment and ill will.

One of the best-known studies to investigate such questions came to a resoundingly negative conclusion. The authors state their claims with a vigor that should give reformers pause. In their important and influential book, *Stealth Democracy*,[6] John Hibbing and Elizabeth Theiss-Morse argue that most Americans dislike politics and actively prefer to leave governance to authoritarian populists and technocrats. When citizens do participate in politics, they typically do so reluctantly, in order to guard against corrupt politicians subverting the public good. On this account, citizens do not participate in more direct or deliberative forums out of an intrinsic interest in politics, but instead only become involved in order to prevent an even worse outcome. If they could trust policymakers to be honest they would eagerly withdraw from politics.

---

[5] Diana C. Mutz, *Hearing the Other Side: Deliberative versus Participatory Democracy* (New York: Cambridge University Press, 2006); and Nina Eliasoph, *Avoiding Politics: How Americans Produce Apathy in Everyday Life* (Cambridge: Cambridge University Press, 1998).

[6] Hibbing and Theiss-Morse, *Stealth Democracy: Americans' Beliefs About How Government Should Work*.

We do not share this view. While it is certainly true that many citizens are averse to participating in the current political system, their frustration with status quo politics does not imply aversion to all forms of political involvement. We argue instead that many citizens today are demobilized precisely because they see the system as driven by blind partisanship, large-donor contributions, insider influence, and special interests. Many citizens would want to participate more in politics if they were given new and constructive ways to engage each other and their representatives. Thus, the directly democratic view and the stealth view of participation directly oppose each other.

WHY DO CITIZENS WITHDRAW FROM POLITICS?

The stealth democracy thesis holds that if citizens believe their representatives can be trusted then the citizens would prefer to withdraw from public life; conversely, if they believe their representatives are corrupt then they will (reluctantly) become more involved. In contrast, we argue that citizens will become more inclined to participate in public life if they perceive the system itself to be more rational and responsive; and conversely, they will become demobilized the more they see the system as rigged.

To get some insight into the stealth thesis, we asked a representative sample of Americans to share their thoughts about participation in directly representative town halls. We administered the survey to a nationally representative sample, asking each citizen two versions of a question about the conditions under which they would be either more or less interested in deliberative participation. Specifically, we asked:

Recently there has been interest in helping regular citizens get more input into the policy process. For example, some organizations run sessions where citizens discuss important issues with their members of Congress. If politics were *more* influenced by self-serving officials and powerful special interests do you think that you would be more or less interested in participating in such a session?

Then we asked a similar question to the survey respondents, but this time proposing politics as "*less* influenced by self-serving officials and powerful special interests." If a citizen reported more interest in participating when corruption is higher, and less interest when it is lower, we categorize that person as having a "stealth" pattern of beliefs, since it fits the expectations of the authors of *Stealth Democracy*. Conversely, we categorize citizens reporting the opposite pattern, as having a "directly representative" set of beliefs. Those who reported the same level of interest either way we categorized as "neutral."

We found that only about 6 percent of citizens held stealth beliefs, while about 66 percent exhibited the directly representative pattern. That is, our respondents were about eleven times more likely to express preferences consistent with the directly representative view than they were with the stealth view. These findings strongly suggest that citizens' frustration with the status quo does *not* imply that they are disinclined to participate in politics *per se*. Instead, it indicates a very widespread interest in alternate methods for creating a more responsive and constructive public dialogue. While it is true that many people find standard partisan politics and interest-group pluralism distasteful, these people tend to see deliberation as an *alternative* to standard forms of participation, and are thus much more open to deliberating than expected.[7]

Our theory does not conceive of deliberation as merely "voting plus" – that is, activities for political junkies akin to attending election rallies or donating to an issue advocacy group. Nor do average citizens regard directly representative democracy in this way. Thus, it would be hasty in the extreme to dismiss directly representative reforms as hopelessly utopian merely because many citizens do not vote, or because they find much about status quo politics distasteful. Directly representative democracy cannot (and should not) do without voting and much of the machinery of current representative democracy: quite the contrary. But rather than thinking of republican consultation and deliberative accountability as, at best, nice frills to add onto interest-group pluralism, we might better think of the deliberative character of a political system as conditioning the very *legitimacy* of standard democratic practices, and creating the conditions for widespread and vibrant citizen participation. As New York governor and reformist presidential candidate Samuel J. Tilden urged, "The means by which a majority comes to be a majority is the more important thing."[8]

---

[7] In practice there is no strict dichotomy between partisan politics and interest-group pluralism on the one hand, and deliberation on the other. We use these two as ideal types. That said, we think that the distinction between, for example, participating in one of our sessions and a partisan rally is sufficiently robust to warrant contrasting the terms without a recurring caveat.

[8] Quoted in John Dewey, *The Public and Its Problems* (Denver, CO: Swallow Press, 1954), 207.

WHO WANTS TO DELIBERATE?

Recall that our first normative criterion for a directly representative innovation is that it gives voice to a wide swath of the public, beyond the partisan activists and organized interest groups that form the backbone of status quo politics. We saw above that most people would want to participate more if they thought politics were less influenced by self-serving officials and powerful special interests. But that finding, in itself, does not guarantee that directly representative institutions would attract new kinds of people into the process at roughly equal rates, nor reveal what kinds of institutions people would like to participate in.

In order to dig deeper into such questions, we recruited a nationally representative sample of citizens to take a survey about hypothetical events of the sort that directly representative reformers envision, asking for their views on different possible designs for town halls. These sessions were hypothetical in the sense that there was no promise or suggestion that the constituent's answer would lead to an invitation to an actual session.

The survey asked about many personal characteristics and attitudes of the respondents. We use the survey to determine whether directly representative events such as our online deliberative town halls are likely to draw a diverse set of constituents. In particular, we examine the kinds of people who indicate a willingness to show up to deliberative events.

We first measured the kinds of individual characteristics that political scientists already use to predict who participates in voting and other aspects of status quo politics: age, race, gender, income, education, partisanship, and the like. We expect that some of the same factors that drive one's willingness to vote, for example, may also drive deliberative participation. Time, money, and education are fairly general resources that make it easier for people to participate. On the other hand, we conceive of directly representative institutions as a partial alternative to traditional partisan politics and interest-group pluralism. Thus, deliberation may be especially motivating to precisely those people for whom traditional participation is relatively unattractive.

Second, since deliberation is very cognitively effortful relative to standard forms of participation, we also include a set of measures that account for the *motivation* to participate in deliberation. Psychologists describe the personality trait *need for cognition* as the extent to which people enjoy effortful cognitive activities, and *need to evaluate* as a disposition to make judgments or take sides.[9] Because several studies show that both the need for cognition and the need to evaluate play an important role in forming and changing attitudes, they are good theoretical candidates for increasing one's willingness to deliberate, and we included standard measures of those on our survey. Similarly, feelings of *political efficacy* might drive a willingness to deliberate. Several studies have shown, unsurprisingly, that feeling confused and powerless in the face of politics is de-motivating. However, deliberative forums are designed to be opportunities to remediate confusion and to provide an alternate channel for involving oneself in politics. Citizens could therefore regard deliberative opportunities as a chance to become more empowered, so we included measures of political efficacy as well. We also included measures of *conflict avoidance*, since critics of deliberation argue that some people are disposed to avoid the inherently contentious give and take of deliberation.

Deliberative democracy aspires to go beyond participation in status quo, power politics. As a result, we also include measures of people's preferences about *democratic processes*. The idea here is that citizens have implicit folk theories about how democracy is supposed to work, and beliefs about how various political processes measure up to those folk philosophies. We include Hibbing and Theiss-Morse's original four *Stealth* democracy survey measures because they were intended to tap such folk intuitions. These are:

[Stealth 1] Elected officials would help the country more if they would stop talking and just take action on important problems. (66% agree)

[Stealth 2] What people call "compromise" in politics is really just selling out one's principles. (43% agree)

[Stealth 3] Our government would run better if decisions were left up to successful business people. (32% agree)

[Stealth 4] Our government would run better if decisions were left up to non-elected, independent experts rather than politicians or the people. (31% agree)

We combine the responses to these four items into a Stealth Democracy index; those who score high on the index are those that most harbor stealth democracy attitudes. We also include an index of people's *trust in government*, because critics of deliberation claim that any apparent interest in more direct democracy is predicated on a lack of trust in current

---

9 John T. Cacioppo, Richard E. Petty, and Chuan Feng Kao. "The efficient assessment of need for cognition," *Journal of Personality Assessment* 48, no. 3 (1984): 306–7; and W. Blair G. Jarvis and Richard E. Petty. "The need to evaluate," *Journal of Personality and Social Psychology* 70, no. 1 (1996): 172.

decision makers. In the Stealth Democracy view, we should observe that those who score high on stealth but low on trust will want to participate, and those high on both will opt out at higher rates. We also include an index we label *sunshine* democracy – a positive rewording of the stealth items (which, we note, all garnered more support in their sunshine form compared to the stealth form).

[Sunshine 1] It is important for elected officials to discuss and debate things thoroughly before making major policy changes. (92% agree)

[Sunshine 2] Openness to other people's views, and a willingness to compromise are important for politics in a country as diverse as ours. (83% agree)

[Sunshine 3] In a democracy like ours, there are some important differences between how government should be run and how a business should be managed. (73% agree)

[Sunshine 4] It is important for the people and their elected representatives to have the final say in running government, rather than leaving it up to unelected experts. (80% agree)

Despite the rather direct content overlap, the sunshine items correlated well with each other, but not with the original stealth items. We therefore created two separate scales: The sunshine items tap how citizens think that representative democracy *should* work in principle, whereas the stealth items tap what they would settle for as a step away from the corrupt status quo.

Finally, we argue that willingness to deliberate is likely to vary according to the institutional characteristics of the deliberative events themselves. There are many ways to construct a town hall. To get a sense of how participation would vary across different types of town halls, we embedded an experiment using the following institutional variations in our survey: (1) the length in time of the deliberative session; (2) whether it was face-to-face or computer mediated; (3) whether the discussion involved an unspecified issue or a specific issue; (4) whether it was conducted only among citizens, or as a consultation with a local official, or as a consultation with their member of Congress; and (5) whether subjects got a monetary incentive to participate.

To implement this experiment on the survey itself, recall that we administered the survey using an online platform, and so we were able to customize the question each participant received by randomly assigning respondents to each of the different variations. Respondents received the following question, but at each place where there are square brackets, the system randomly substituted one of the options within the brackets without showing the brackets or the other options (and when the option was <none> the system left that space blank).

Recently there has been interest in helping regular citizens get more input into the policy process. For example, many organizations run [*one day / one hour*] sessions where citizens [*come together / use the Internet*] to discuss [*important issues / immigration policy*] [*<none>; with local officials; with their member of Congress*].*[<none>; Participants get $25 as thanks for their involvement.*]
    If you had the chance to participate in such a session, how interested do you think you would be in doing so: (5) Extremely interested; (4) Quite interested; (3) Somewhat interested; (2) Not too interested; (1) Not at all interested

For example, respondents who were randomized to see the last option in each of the five brackets would see:

Recently there has been interest in helping regular citizens get more input into the policy process. For example, many organizations run one hour sessions where citizens use the Internet to discuss immigration policy with their member of Congress. Participants get $25 as thanks for their involvement. If you had the chance to participate in such a session, how interested do you think you would be in doing so?

In this sort of survey experiment, the respondent would only get this one version of the question, and would not know that other respondents were receiving different versions of the same question. We then use their responses to see what characteristics make them more likely to want to participate in a town hall, and specifically what kind of session they are most likely to want to participate in. We simply compared who expressed the highest interest among the survey respondents across the five design categories.
    Some of these institutional features should have predictable effects on citizens' willingness to participate. People are busy and politics takes time, so it seems obvious to test for sensitivity to the time necessary to participate (the first option) as well as to monetary incentives (the fifth option). Computer-mediated deliberation (the second option) is generally more convenient, certainly for those who have access to the Internet, and greatly reduces travel and logistical costs. Moreover, it accommodates geographically disparate participants. In addition, the relative buffer of mediated deliberation may mitigate reluctance to deliberate among those who dislike conflict or prefer partial anonymity.
    We included a general-versus-specific topic variation (the third option) to see if rates of interest in deliberation are predicated on people imagining

the topics that most interest them. Under an interest-group pluralism frame, we should not be surprised to find that participation is linked to particular interests. Deliberative theory, however, predicts somewhat weaker effects because we have reasons to participate even when we do not have a large, direct stake in a particular outcome.

Finally, there are both theoretical and practical differences between deliberation among fellow citizens (i.e., horizontal deliberation), versus citizens and their elected representatives (i.e., republican consultation and deliberative accountability), so we randomized the type of session (the fourth option).

We should note that absolute levels of interest in deliberative participation were quite high. A large majority of people (83 percent) expressed at least some interest in participating in a deliberative session. Combining across the various conditions, 27 percent said that they would be "extremely" interested in participating, another 27 percent said they would be "quite" interested, and 29 percent "somewhat" interested. Twelve percent said they were "not too interested," and only 5 percent said that they were "not at all" interested.

We next examine the characteristics and attitudes of our survey respondents to see the types of people who report that they are likely to show up at each of the different institutional settings. The desire to "get more input into the policy process" appears to differ in its predictors relative to partisan politics and interest-group pluralism. Of the seven demographic characteristics that predict standard participation (such as voting and contributing money to campaigns), only education points in the same direction as those associated with greater participation in partisan politics or interest-group pluralism (and even so, it is weaker than in predicting voting).

Younger people, racial minorities, and lower income people expressed significantly *more* willingness to deliberate, all of which are reversals from traditional participation patterns. Women, less partisan people, and non-church goers were also slightly more likely to want to deliberate. On these criteria, it appears that the kinds of people attracted to the deliberative opportunities offered are distinct from those drawn to partisan politics and interest-group pluralism. These results are consistent with directly representative democracy's aspiration to provide an outlet for those frustrated with the options available to them under status quo politics.

There were fewer surprises for motivation. General political interest, need for cognition, need to evaluate, and conflict avoidance all pointed in the expected direction. Efficacy had a small, negative association. Unsurprisingly, people were also attracted by a monetary incentive. More surprisingly, people did not seem especially sensitive to the length, mode, or specificity of the deliberative session. This last finding suggests that, contrary to an interest-group politics frame, people are not especially parochial in their willingness to deliberate.

Most people were motivated by the thought of talking with a high-ranking government official, so there seems to be somewhat more enthusiasm for vertical (i.e., republican) deliberation than horizontal deliberation only among fellow citizens. Sunshine and trust were not powerful predictors of wanting to participate. However, we do see that people who score high on stealth were not as attracted as were others by the *hypothetical* prospect of talking with their (presumptively corrupt) members of Congress.

Overall, these findings present quite a different picture of willingness to deliberate than what we might have expected if we thought of deliberation as just another form of traditional political participation. But it could be that the responses to our hypothetical survey are just cheap talk – that those who say they will show up to a hypothetical event are not necessarily those who actually show up to a real one. Or alternatively, it may be that respondents might react differently to an actual invitation from the representative, an outreach effort that might be counter to their stereotype of typical politicians. So, we now turn to comparing these results on interest in hypothetical deliberation with those analyzing actual behavior in response to our real deliberative town halls.

WHO ACTUALLY SHOWS UP TO DELIBERATE?

While our study of the online deliberative town halls was designed as a research project, in practice it was an intervention in the real world of democratic politics – actual members of Congress interacted with actual constituents – and so our study gives us a chance to examine the kinds of people who actually show up when given an opportunity to participate in directly representative democracy. That is, we were able to observe which cross section of citizens chose to participate in the alternate democratic reality that we created, within town halls that are designed to foster constructive engagement among citizens and between citizens and their member of Congress. As with any invitation, some of those we invited to participate showed up to the event, while others did not. Thus, we are able to examine the pattern of who participated in our event as a way to address our first normative criterion for directly representative institutions – whether our deliberative town halls promote political equality by attracting a broad cross section of the community.

Among those constituents we contacted for the study, about 65 percent indicated that they were both interested in participating in an online deliberative town hall with their member of Congress, *and* were also available to attend the meeting at a specific date and time.[10] Those who indicated an ability to participate in the event at the stated time were eligible to receive an invitation. We randomly assigned invitations by lottery to the eligible participants, and among those who received an invitation 34 percent ended up participating in one of our deliberative town halls.

And who showed up to our sessions? First, as in the hypothetical study, our findings show that the people who are *less likely* to participate in standard politics – such as voting or making campaign contributions – were the ones who were equally or even *more likely* to participate in our deliberative town halls. In particular, we found that our directly representative events tended to attract lower income participants and those with less steady employment, which strongly dispels the notion that deliberation only attracts those at the top of the income distribution. While not statistically significant, citizens' age, race, gender, and strength of partisanship, as in the hypothetical case, reversed the pattern associated with traditional political participation; that is, the evidence suggests that nonpartisans, racial minorities, women, and younger participants were *more likely* to show up than their counterparts, perhaps because the ease of access was especially important to them.

Far from being only political junkies, we find that the *participants in our sessions were more representative of eligible voters than actual voters.* That is, not everyone who can vote does, and the ones who do are not a random draw of those who can – they are biased toward being wealthier, more educated, etc. In general, the folks who participated in our sessions were less biased on most criteria than those who vote. Moreover, nearly all of the biases we did have reversed those from standard participation. In short, our sessions brought new kinds of citizens into the political process.

---

[10] Our recruitment design did not separate those who were unwilling to participate from those who wanted to participate but had a conflict with the set time for the deliberative town hall. It is not inconceivable that many of the 35 percent who declined participation did so because of scheduling conflicts rather than lack of interest.

Beyond demographics, we also found that conflict-averse citizens were less likely to show up, while those who had a stronger sense of self-efficacy, those who paid close attention to the issue of immigration, and those who followed politics more generally were more likely to show up. Finally, those who score high on all three of our process measures (sunshine, trust, and stealth) were more likely to participate in our sessions than those who score low on each. It should not surprise us that citizens who score high on sunshine also tend to participate in deliberation; the same for trust, given our results about the sources of withdrawal above. However, the stealth finding is the opposite of our finding in the hypothetical conditions, which, at first, seems quite surprising. Why might respondents who say politicians should discuss issues less and compromise less, and operate government more like an unaccountable business, be more likely to show up to a deliberative town hall? Why should all of our important results between the hypothetical and actual conditions be replicated except this one?

In the hypothetical case, those who were high on the *Stealth* index were especially unlikely to want to participate in the deliberative town hall involving a member of Congress. Yet here we get a complete reversal. Those high on the *Stealth* index were especially likely to want to participate in our sessions that were hosted by their member of Congress. On the skeptic's view, this stark reversal is difficult to explain. Indeed, that *sunshine* and *stealth* attitudes should pull powerfully in the same direction is perplexing at first blush. The two sets of questions were explicitly designed to point in opposite directions in their content.

However, if we question the standard interpretation of the *Stealth* measure, the results become less perplexing. On the standard interpretation of *Stealth*, most people dislike politics intrinsically, do not want to be more involved, but reluctantly agree to more direct democracy as a hedge against the corrupt status quo. They would most prefer a nondemocratic technocracy that operates in the background. Recognizing that this ideal, technocratic model might not be achievable, they settle for more referenda and other forms of direct democratic control.

We agree with the skeptics that most citizens prefer stealth democracy to direct democracy, and more direct democracy to the status quo. However, the concept of directly representative democracy extends by one step the same move that the skeptics make regarding direct democracy. That is, just as with the apparent desire for more direct democracy, people do not really hold stealth democracy as their first preference. Instead, they will settle for stealth democracy if the civics textbook version of directly representative democracy is not achievable.

With this expanded menu in view, we can see why *Stealth* reverses its effect between the hypothetical and actual offer to deliberate. The actual offer from their member of Congress communicates new information about that representative that runs counter to their stereotypes of politicians. Constituents might believe, in the abstract, that most members of Congress are corrupt politicians who do not really care about what average citizens think. But when their own representative contacts them and, in effect, says, *"No, really, I do want to talk with you. Will two weeks from Tuesday at 7pm work?"* they update their beliefs about what their representative is really like. The frustration and desire for reform evinced by stealth attitudes indicate motivation for change, rather than apathy or aversion.

CONCLUSION

Many people are initially skeptical about directly representative democracy. The story goes that average citizens hate politics and cannot even get it right when they show up every four years (if they show up) to cast a vote on a simple choice between candidates, about whom the media have been bombarding them with information for months. How can anyone seriously expect them to want to participate in more detailed discussion of policy, much less to do so with sufficient information and competence?

The intuition behind such skepticism is reasonable. However, our aspirations for directly representative reform do not seem so hopelessly utopian when we consider that many citizens are demobilized precisely by the peculiarities of partisan and interest-group politics that critics mistakenly take as the practical limits of political participation in a contemporary mass democracy. People's willingness to engage in republican consultation and deliberative accountability is much higher than previously thought, and those most willing to engage are precisely those turned off by standard partisan and interest-group politics.

So our deliberative town hall sessions would seem to pass our first test for improving democracy – promoting an equal voice for a wide cross-section of citizens. Of course, this chapter has only focused on the first step in participation by examining who actually shows up. What remains for us to show is what our participants do once they show up. We find widespread and equal participation across our participants, from the amount of knowledge they gain, to how robust and effectively they participate during the sessions. Overall, far from rendering directly representative reforms ridiculous or perverse on their own terms, these findings suggest that the directly representative approach embodies opportunities for practical reform quite congruent with the aspirations of academics and average citizens alike.

4

Rational Ignorance and Reasonable Learning

Being ignorant is not so much a shame as being unwilling to learn.
—Benjamin Franklin, *Poor Richard's Almanac*

Most democratic citizens are remarkably ignorant about politics and policy. On survey after survey, across time and context, large numbers of people cannot correctly answer seemingly basic questions about government. It might seem unrealistic in the extreme, then, to think that ordinary citizens could engage constructively in republican consultation and deliberative accountability even if they wanted to. Skeptics argue that proposals like ours are, in the words of Judge Richard Posner, "purely aspirational and unrealistic ... with ordinary people having as little interest in complex policy issues as they have aptitude for them."[1]

Notice that this criticism, if true, is even more damning than the *Stealth Democracy* argument from the previous chapter. Stealth democrats only claim that citizens are reluctant to participate in democratic politics. Here the critics claim that even in the (unlikely) event that citizens show up for a directly representative forum, they will simply not have the knowledge or capacity to participate in any meaningful way. If these critics are right, our second criterion for directly representative forums – fostering adequate learning to enable meaningful participation – will be difficult to achieve.

In contrast to this more cynical view of democracy, we claim that when legislators engage in substantive communication with their constituents,

[1] Richard A. Posner, *Law, Pragmatism, and Democracy* (Cambridge, MA: Harvard University Press, 2005), 107.

they provide both the motive and the opportunity for citizens to become informed about politics. With Franklin, we argue that there is little problem with *ex ante* ignorance just so long as there is a willingness to learn. In our study, we find this capacity to become informed is often latent – i.e., lying dormant until the proper conditions for it to become manifest present themselves. This capacity is nonetheless real, widely spread throughout the mass public, and becomes activated when meaningful opportunities to participate, like our sessions, arise. That is to say, citizens may be ignorant under status quo politics, but we find they are willing to learn in order to facilitate directly representative democracy.

We assess these claims with evidence from our experiments.[2] We find that the constituents who participated in our deliberative town halls demonstrated a vibrant capacity to become informed in response to the opportunities presented by our sessions. Citizens gained knowledge primarily by increasing their attention to policy *outside* the context of the experiment, rather than from the information within the sessions themselves. They were more motivated to pay attention to politics and policy knowing that their elected officials really were going to listen to what they had to say. Moreover, all kinds of citizens exhibited this capacity for policy learning; it was unrelated to people's prior political knowledge. As we showed in Chapter 3, a wide cross section of citizens is interested in participating in directly representative institutions. In this chapter we show a similarly wide cross section of citizens exercise their capacity to become informed.

MEANS, MOTIVES, AND OPPORTUNITIES TO BECOME INFORMED ABOUT POLITICS

Survey researchers have studied citizens' political knowledge extensively, with most presuming that, in order to be effective participants in their own self-government, citizens must have specific factual knowledge of the government's structure, processes, politics, and policies available for recall at any given time. This implicit working theory of democracy among survey researchers is itself rooted in the status quo of modern mass democracy, where citizens are policy consumers. They need to know

---

[2] This chapter is largely based on our article, Kevin M. Esterling, Michael A. Neblo, and David M. J. Lazer, "Means, Motive, and Opportunity in Becoming Informed about Politics: A Deliberative Field Experiment Involving Members of Congress and Their Constituents," *Public Opinion Quarterly* 75, no. 3 (Fall 2011): 483–503.

a lot about numerous pending issues, and the specific actions their elected representatives have taken.

Collecting and memorizing this level of factual detail would be extremely taxing for anyone but the most dedicated political junkie, and as we know, most citizens typically do not make the effort. Researchers in this tradition are not surprised by these findings, since the status quo of today's politics creates little motivation for the average citizen to learn much. On their account, having little to no knowledge of politics is quite understandable. Indeed, it is rational and sensible, since it is time consuming and effortful for citizens to follow the news and become informed.

In the traditional view of survey research, when citizens choose not to become informed about politics, they effectively free ride on the efforts of others who do learn about elected officials and hold them accountable for their actions. As a result, citizens' lack of political knowledge drives both inequality, because it is mostly the highly advantaged who typically read the newspapers and weigh in, and democratic failure, because there is too little consultation and accountability overall. In effect, this research tradition envisions a democracy that has high informational barriers to entry to a system that invites only a low level of involvement and reward.[3]

In contrast, on the directly representative view, we claim that it is citizens' often latent willingness and capacity to learn that is necessary to make republican consultation and deliberative accountability effective. Citizens do not need to know about policies and political actions at all times or to recall such information when they happen to be dialed up by the survey researcher. Instead, for directly representative consultation and accountability to be effective, elected officials must believe that citizens will become informed about policies and about their actions when citizens have a *reason* to become informed. That is, republican consultation and deliberative accountability only require citizens to have the *capacity* to learn about a topic, and to be *willing* to exercise that capacity when given a relevant opportunity.

We argue that the republican consultation or deliberative accountability within a directly representative event creates both a motivation as well as an opportunity for citizens to become informed. When citizens know they will have an opportunity to interact with their elected officials and fellow citizens within a deliberative town hall, they seek out information to enable their own effective participation, and they more deeply engage

[3] Michael X. Delli Carpini and Scott Keeter, *What Americans Know about Politics and Why It Matters* (New Haven, CT: Yale University Press, 1996).

that information. That is, they will engage in reasonable learning. From this perspective, the relevant measure of political knowledge centers on the *willingness and capacity* for citizens to become informed when given a reason to do so, rather than the standing knowledge they happen to recall when dialed up by a survey researcher. In contrast to the anemic view of democratic participation that is implicitly embraced by many survey researchers, our vision of democracy offers citizens a relatively low barrier to entry for an opportunity to participate at a high level of involvement and reward.

Each vision of democracy lends itself to a distinct method for measuring political knowledge. The standard view values memorized facts, and so the appropriate method to assess such knowledge is a survey administered to citizens in the form of a "pop quiz." The pop quiz method embeds political knowledge questions within a survey that is administered at an arbitrary place and time.[4]

In contrast, the directly representative approach administers a survey at the moment that a citizen *has a reason to be informed*, such as at a town hall event, focusing on the constituent's knowledge gain from before to after the event. This capacity to become informed cannot be captured in standard surveys since pop quiz surveys are not timed to coincide with a meaningful event. We instead use methods that measure the capacity of respondents to become informed rather than what happens to be stored in a citizen's memory at a random moment in time.[5]

To directly representative democrats, ordinary citizens' so called "rational ignorance" about politics is less a matter of willful free riding than a perception that staying informed about politics benefits no one in today's world. If citizens perceive politics as largely a matter of interest-group power and partisan bloodsport, then there is little reason for them to expend the effort on a rigged game. But in the view of directly representative democrats, expanding opportunities to participate through new technology means that politics need not involve only elites. If citizens perceive they have an opportunity to engage with their representative in

---

[4] For example, see Michael X. Delli Carpini and Scott Keeter, "Measuring Political Knowledge: Putting First Things First," *American Journal of Political Science* 37, no. 4 (November 1993): 1179–206.

[5] Arthur Lupia and James N. Druckman, "Preference Change in Competitive Political Environments," *Annual Review of Political Science* 19, no. 1 (2016): 13–31; and Betsy Sparrow, Jenny Liu, and Daniel M. Wegner, "Google effects on memory: Cognitive consequences of having information at our fingertips," *Science* 333, no. 6043 (2011): 776–8.

a substantively meaningful way, they are more apt to become informed in order to participate effectively. That citizens currently invest little time and energy in learning about status quo politics, to decide which checks to write and which votes to cast, does not imply that in a more deliberative system they would not do better. Instead, citizens need a more persuasive set of motives and opportunities to become informed, and as we show, when those opportunities arise, ordinary citizens really are capable of gaining the knowledge appropriate for consulting with elected officials and holding them accountable.

JUST THE FACTS

We assess the extent to which participants in our online deliberative town halls gained knowledge about the topic under consideration, US immigration policy, and hence whether they met our second criterion for the forums constituting a democratic improvement. Among the participants in our study, we randomly assigned whether or not they received an invitation to attend a deliberative town hall. On the follow up survey, we administered a battery of questions that measured their knowledge of immigration policy. Random assignment allows us to measure constituents' knowledge gains on our survey, comparing knowledge levels among those who attended the online deliberative town halls with that of an equivalent group of constituents who did not attend one.

As we saw in Figure 2.2, our study design provided reading materials to the study participants who were randomly assigned to either the information only or to the deliberative group conditions, but we did not provide reading material to those in our true control condition. This setup allows us to test whether respondents who participated in the online deliberative town halls gained more policy knowledge than those who either just read the materials or were asked the immigration policy knowledge questions cold. Since the deliberative condition bundles reading material with the opportunity to participate, it provides both the means and the motivation for participants to learn. The information only treatment provides citizens the means but not the motivation for knowledge acquisition. The true control condition provides neither.

Several days before each deliberative town hall, we administered a survey that contained background reading materials on the issue. The survey only went to participants assigned to the deliberative and information groups. These readings described basic facts about US immigration

and policy in effect at the time of the study (the summer of 2006). We
adapted the background information from Congressional Research
Service and Congressional Budget Office reports, and scaled it to a ninth-
grade reading level. All of the congressional offices that participated, both
Republicans and Democrats, agreed on the content. See the appendix to
this chapter for a copy of the background readings.

In both the baseline and follow up surveys we included the questions
found in Table 4.1. The background information contained, but did not
highlight, the answers to these questions. Importantly, the participants
were not informed that they would be tested on their knowledge of the
issue before, during, or after the event, so they did not know to read up on
immigration in anticipation of the test that we would later administer.[6]

REASONABLE LEARNING

As we mentioned earlier, citizens do poorly on "pop quiz" knowledge
surveys. The baseline survey that we administered at the outset of our
study also contained the set of immigration policy knowledge questions,
administered without context and with no reason for respondents to
know the answers. As expected our respondents showed very low levels
of initial knowledge in this pop quiz. On most of the items, citizens did
not perform much better than what one would see if they were merely
guessing at the answers. Of the six questions, on only one did participants
answer significantly above the guess rate, and for three questions, participants did significantly worse than if they had just randomly guessed.
From our point of view, these inaccurate responses to the knowledge
items on the baseline survey are no surprise since they are administered
in an informational vacuum, prior to the opportunity to participate in a
deliberative town hall.

The story is very different, however, when we look at the follow-up
survey that we administered shortly after the conclusion of each deliberative town hall. Table 4.1 displays the results. The true control citizens
who did not receive the background readings did no better than on the
baseline survey. So it appears that intervening events between the baseline and follow up survey, such as a major news story, did not cause the

---

[6] In all, 2,222 constituents participated in the study, and of these 437 read the background
material *and* attended an online deliberative town hall with their representative, 528 read
the background reading material but did not participate in an online deliberative town
hall, and 1,257 served as true controls.

TABLE 4.1. *Immigration policy knowledge questions posttest*

Question	Responses	Percent correct by group
Q1 About how many illegal immigrants currently reside in the United States?	a) 100,000 b) 4,000,000 c) **12,000,000** d) 23,000,000 e) 96,000,000 f) Don't Know	DG: 41 IO: 33 TC: 33
Q2 About how many illegal immigrants come into the United States each year?	a) 50,000 b) 200,000 c) **500,000** d) 2,000,000 e) 10,000,000 f) Don't Know	DG: 35 IO: 24 TC: 18
Q3 About what fraction of illegal immigrants in the United States are from Mexico?	a) Less than ¼ b) Between ⅓ and ½ c) **Between ½ and ⅔** d) About ¾ e) More than ¾ f) Don't Know	DG: 37 IO: 20 TC: 24
Q4 Under current law, is it a felony to reside illegally in the United States?	a) Yes b) **No** c) Don't Know	DG: 47 IO: 41 TC: 33
Q5 Under current law, do companies who want to employ noncitizen immigrants have to prove that doing so will not hurt the employment of US citizens?	a) **Yes** b) No c) Don't Know	DG: 37 IO: 34 TC: 27
Q6 Under current law, are illegal immigrants who have lived in the United States for five years or more eligible to apply for citizenship?	a) Yes b) **No** c) Don't Know	DG: 61 IO: 42 TC: 40

Note: **Boldface** *font indicates the correct answer.* The "Percent correct by group" column reports the "intention to treat" effects (see the appendix for a fuller explanation); all comparisons statistically significant under the chi square test of independence.

knowledge gains that we see in the other conditions. A gain that would have been due to such an outside event would be reflected among the true controls as well. The information only group did learn from the reading materials, as they did have higher rates of correct answers on all of the questions. However, the deliberative group (DG) gained even more, with higher rates of correct answers on all of the questions than the information group (IO), and much higher than the true controls (TC).

We also conducted more sophisticated analyses to make sure that the deliberative participants processed the policy information more deeply than those for whom we merely provided information without a strong reason to learn it. We combined the six immigration policy knowledge questions to get an overall measure, and then compared the deliberative group to the information only group. We saw a substantial increase in the policy knowledge of deliberative participants. For example, the change in knowledge from participating in a deliberative town hall would move someone who begins at the 50th percentile up to the 63rd percentile. Comparing those who participated in the online deliberative town halls to those who were in our true control group doubled the effect, representing a change from the 50th percentile to the 73rd percentile on policy knowledge.

Recall that we conducted this study as a randomized experiment, as described in Chapter 2, so these changes are likely causal effects (for more technical details on our statistical analysis, see the methods appendix at the end of the book). That is, participating in our online deliberative town halls actually seems to cause the participants to learn. Standard political knowledge surveys just do not measure the latent capacity of citizens to become informed when given the means and motive to do so. Our results show that participants in our deliberative town halls respond to the opportunities we created to become better informed about immigration policy, demonstrating that our deliberative town halls met our second aspiration for directly representative democracy.

A RISING TIDE

Might these deliberative town halls, however, widen knowledge inequalities that already exist among citizens? Some worry that deliberative democracy might inadvertently make the inequalities between more and less advantaged citizens worse, rather than lessening them. Do already knowledgeable individuals benefit disproportionately from these deliberative town halls, or does a rising tide lift all boats? Unsurprisingly, standard surveys do find a strong relationship between a respondent's general knowledge of politics and knowledge of issue-specific facts. This might suggest that those with the highest general knowledge will also have the largest policy knowledge gains, since having extensive political knowledge may make it easier for respondents to learn new information.

But this relationship does not establish whether the same pattern will hold when citizens have the means, motives, and opportunity to become informed. To answer this question, we measured people's general political knowledge, and found that those with higher levels of general political knowledge did *not* learn disproportionately more from the sessions. Instead, we observe the capacity to gain new knowledge across a wide cross section of citizens. This should not come as a surprise given the findings in Chapter 3 that the intrinsic interest in directly representative democracy is widely shared. Thus, our online sessions promote *equal participation* by equipping all participants with knowledge that can empower them to participate effectively.

TEACHING TO THE TEST?

Participating in the deliberative town halls clearly increased people's knowledge regarding the issue. But what, exactly, about the deliberative town hall caused these gains? Interestingly, we found no direct teaching effect from the sessions themselves. We counted the number of times that a correct answer to the questions came up in each session and found that constituents in sessions with more of this factual information did not do appreciably better on the information questions. So the citizens had to be learning more *outside* of the sessions. But how and why?

To puzzle this out we first test to see whether there is a treatment effect on participants that enhances their *motivation* to attend to information outside the confines of our experiment, and we then test whether attending to external information increases immigration policy knowledge. We have two good candidates for measures of the motivation to attend to information outside the experiment. The first is people's response to the statement, "It is a citizen's duty to keep informed about politics even if it is time consuming." The second is the extent to which people talked about immigration policy outside of the experiment itself.

We find that those in the deliberative group were 11 percent more likely than those in the information-only group to believe it is their duty to keep informed about politics and 6 percent more than the true controls. We also find that those in the deliberation group were 9 percent more likely to discuss immigration policy knowledge outside the experiment when compared to the information-only group, and 15 percent more likely than the true controls.

Now consider the second step, whether attending to external information enhances policy knowledge. We find that having immigration policy discussant partners outside the experiment translated into learning, but only for those who participated in the deliberative sessions. Among deliberators, having discussant partners on immigration policy increased immigration policy knowledge by about 15 percent, but among those who did not participate in a deliberative town hall, the number of discussion partners was unrelated to learning. Similarly, the substantive effect of an increased duty to keep informed closely paralleled the results regarding immigration discussants, though they were somewhat less statistically significant.

We take these results to indicate that the deliberative session enhanced citizens' motivation to attend to information outside the experiment broadly, with discussion partners as only one of many possible external sources of policy information. It also suggests that these deliberative town halls might have ramifications for citizens beyond those in the sessions themselves, a question to which we return in Chapter 7.

CONCLUSION

The pessimistic conclusions drawn from survey research on political knowledge follow in large part from the assessment methods themselves, since they fail to capture the dynamics of what motivates learning. The problem with citizen knowledge has less to do with the inadequacy of democratic citizens and more with the inadequacy of survey researchers' implicit theory of democracy, and their corresponding method of administering a contextless pop quiz. The latent capacity to become informed about policy is central to our directly representative vision of democracy. Our experiment demonstrates that citizens have a capacity to become informed, and that they are willing to exercise this capacity when given a motive and opportunity. Indeed, it appears that deliberation itself can create a motivation to learn, and that well-designed deliberative events can help all kinds of citizens better discharge their civic duties.[7]

---

[7] Phillip E. Tetlock, Linda Skitka, and Richard Boettger, "Social and Cognitive Strategies for Coping with Accountability: Conformity, Complexity, and Bolstering," *Journal of Personality and Social Psychology* 57, no. 4 (1989): 632–40.

We have reason to believe that this capacity to become informed is not limited to the confines of our experiment; members of Congress themselves believe that citizens exercise this capacity often enough to maintain real accountability in practice.[8] In this sense, our hopes for a more directly representative democracy are on a stronger footing than might be suggested by standard studies of political knowledge. Directly democratic opportunities like our online deliberative town halls can pave the way for citizens to interact with their member of Congress and other publicly accountable actors more regularly. Doing so would afford citizens more opportunities to exercise their capacity to learn about politics and policy, and so better approximate widely shared goals for a knowledgeable and engaged democratic citizenry.

This chapter demonstrates that the design of our online deliberative town halls met the second requirement of a well-designed directly representative democratic institution: it facilitated constituents learning how to participate meaningfully and constructively in republican consultation and deliberative accountability. We build on the argument we set out in previous chapters, where we argued that directly representative democracy is based on a very different conception of political legitimacy than the "parties and interest groups" model of contemporary democracy. Both here and in Chapter 3, we find that participants in our directly representative town halls respond in a manner that is far more consistent with the normative expectations for democratic citizens than is typically the case in modern mass democracies.

Whether these knowledge gains are enough to underwrite high quality engagement with their elected representatives remains an open question, however. In the next chapter we assess the quality of the discourse at our events, and whether and how our sessions changed participants' hearts and minds.

APPENDIX: IMMIGRATION BACKGROUND MATERIALS

Please carefully read the following background information about immigration in the United States. Afterwards you'll have the chance to provide your opinions on this topic.

---

[8] R. Douglas Arnold, *The Logic of Congressional Action* (New Haven, CT: Yale University Press, 1992), 68; Fenno, *Home Style: House Members in Their Districts,* 231; and John W. Kingdon, *Congressmen's Voting Decisions* (Ann Arbor: University of Michigan Press, 1989), 248.

INTRODUCTION

Noncitizens can enter the United States legally on a permanent basis, or on a temporary basis. If a person is granted permission to come into the country permanently, he or she is known as a legal immigrant and gets a "green card." In 2004, 362,000 people came into the United States this way. After five years, if they learn English and meet other conditions, legal immigrants can become citizens. About 537,000 people completed the process to earn citizenship in 2004. Noncitizens can also enter the country on a temporary visa, as a tourist, student, or temporary worker. These visitors are not expected to stay beyond the term of their visas. Anyone without a green card or a current visa is considered an illegal immigrant.

ILLEGAL IMMIGRANTS

About 12 million illegal immigrants live in the United States, according to recent estimates. Every year, about half a million (500,000) new illegal immigrants enter the country. Between half and two-thirds come from Mexico. Sometimes crossing the border can be dangerous. Smugglers known as "coyotes" often use unsafe methods to sneak their customers across the border. The US Border Patrol believes that nearly two thousand people died trying to cross the border between 1998 and 2004.

California is home to the largest number of illegal immigrants, followed by Texas, Florida, New York, Arizona, Illinois, New Jersey, and North Carolina. Illegal immigrants can be deported if they are caught. In 2004, 1.2 million were caught; some left voluntarily while others were deported. Deporting illegal immigrants can be complicated if the immigrants have children who were born in the United States, because under current law, these children are legal citizens, even if their parents are not.

ECONOMIC IMPLICATIONS

People are often concerned about how illegal immigration affects the job market, as well as taxes and social services like healthcare and education.

Right now, illegal immigrants make up about 5 percent of the US workforce. Many immigrants work in textiles, food manufacturing, construction, agriculture, food services, and janitorial services, where they earn 27 percent less than US citizens with similar education and experience in the same industries. About 75 percent of the illegal immigrant population works. While it is very difficult to say with precision how illegal immigration affects wages, a report by the Congressional Budget Office suggests that it primarily affects American workers without high school diplomas. The wages for such jobs go down (by about 4 percent), which hurts these workers, but raises profits for American employers and businesses, and lowers prices for American consumers. Immigrants are consumers too, who pay for American products when they are here, so they contribute to the economy in that way as well. And some argue that immigration encourages American workers to invest in education to compete for higher wage jobs.

TAXES AND SOCIAL SERVICES

It is also difficult to know exactly how illegal immigration affects taxes and social services. Although many illegal workers pay social security and other taxes, they are not eligible for many government benefits. On the other hand, over a quarter of illegal immigrants live in poverty. Many use emergency health care, and their children attend US schools (although some of those children were born here, and so are legal citizens who are entitled to public school education).

LEGISLATIVE EFFORTS

Taking on the issue of illegal immigration, both the House of Representatives and the Senate have passed legislation in recent months. The bills are very different, and in order to pass a law to set immigration policy, the two houses must come up with one bill that will pass in both chambers. Then the President must sign the bill to establish new immigration law.

The Senate bill, called the Comprehensive Immigration Reform Act of 2006, contains a path for illegal immigrants to become permanent residents if they pay a fine and go through a process to qualify as legal citizens. The bill also grants more visas to immigrants coming to work in certain industries where demand for their labor is higher (guest workers). Under current law, an American company who wants to use foreign workers under such programs must prove that doing so will not hurt the employment of current US citizens.

The House of Representatives bill, called the Border Protection, Anti-terrorism, and Illegal Immigration Control Act of 2005, makes it a felony to be in the United States without proper documentation. Under this proposal, anyone who knowingly helps illegal immigrants can be prosecuted for a felony as well.

DETAILS OF THE SENATE BILL

Temporary Guest Worker Program When certain industries have high demand for workers, this bill sets up temporary visas for workers to come to this country to get jobs in those industries. These guest workers must have a job lined up before they enter the country. They can stay up to three years, and can bring their families with them. No illegal immigrants currently living and working in the United States would be eligible for this program. For the first year, 325,000 workers could enter the country under this program. After that, the number would be adjusted every year, depending on the demand for workers in each industry.

    Path to Citizenship Illegal immigrants currently in the United States are not eligible for the guest worker program, but they may be allowed to become legal permanent residents. The bill sets up three different categories of illegal immigrants: those who have been in the country five years or more, those who have been here for two to five years, and those who have been here less than two years. The immigrants who have been here longest, since 2001 or earlier, can become permanent residents if they have been working for at least three of the five years. They have to pay a $5,000 fine. Their spouses and children will also get green cards. Once they have their green cards, they can eventually become citizens if they decide to go through that process too. Immigrants who came after 2001 and before 2004 (have been here two to five years) can get permission to stay and work for three years, provided they also pay a fine, of $1,000, and have been working already for the last two years. With their new three-year visa, they can apply for other visas that allow for longer stays. To do this, they have to go to a point of entry on the border and file their application there.

    Immigrants who have been in the United States less than two years will not receive any opportunities in the guest worker programs or paths to citizenship. They have to go back to their countries of origin and compete for a visa like everyone else.

    Employer Sanctions Under the Senate bill, fines for employers who knowingly hire illegal immigrants would be raised from their current amounts to $20,000. Repeat offenders would get jail time. Within eighteen months, all employers would be required to use a database to verify that their employees are legal.

Border security This bill would call for 370 miles of fencing along the United States-Mexico border, and another 500 miles of vehicle barriers. The Border Patrol, which has 11,000 agents right now, would be increased by 1,000 agents right away, and by 14,000 by 2011, for a total of 25,000 agents. The National Guard currently assists at the border, but under this bill, there would be a limit of twenty-one days to National Guard assignments there, to free up Guard troops when they are needed elsewhere.

English as the national language The Senate bill establishes English as the official national language of the United States.

DETAILS OF THE HOUSE BILL

Border Security The House Bill provides money for guarding the border with satellites, sensors in the ground, cameras, and radar. It also calls for 700 miles of fences along the United States-Mexico border, and more border patrol agents to patrol the fences.

Illegal entry and smuggling Anyone caught smuggling illegal immigrants into the country can be prosecuted for aggravated felony charges, and could face mandatory minimum prison sentences. The bill also makes it a felony to be in the United States illegally. Immigrants face prison for entering the United States without proper documentation, and those who do so more than once face mandatory minimum prison sentences. People who marry illegal immigrants to help them get green cards face criminal penalties. So does anyone else who helps an illegal immigrant commit immigration fraud.

Employer sanctions The House bill calls for fines of as much as $40,000 each time an employer hires an undocumented worker. Repeat offenders could face as much as thirty years of prison time. Within six years, employers would have to use a database to check Social Security numbers for each employee.

5

(The) Deliberative Persuasion

> The best argument against democracy is a five-minute conversation with the average voter.
>
> —Winston Churchill

Perhaps surprisingly, we agree with Churchill's observation. If you ask voters individually for off-the-cuff reactions to complex policy questions without any context, you will often get responses ill-suited to good democratic governance. But as we showed in the previous chapter the method is just as much the problem as the people. One of the best arguments *for* democracy is a fifty-minute conversation *among* average voters. The deliberative context makes all the difference.

Town halls stand as perhaps the central and most concrete example of *potentially* deliberative interactions between elected officials and their constituents. The folk image is familiar: the member of Congress back home in the district, standing in the front of a community meeting room filled with constituents listening to the representative earnestly explaining her Washington activities. The representative and constituents engage in direct exchange about national policies and priorities. While that folk image may not be manifest in current practices of consultation, we believe that it can be made more so, and that moving in that direction can set off a virtuous circle of expectations and practices. Experiencing deliberative persuasion in politics is apt to make one open to deliberation as a mode of politics – that is, to be of the deliberative persuasion.

Despite the centrality of town halls in the everyday depiction of representative consultation, it turns out that very little is known in the political science literature about what actually happens in these meetings, and in particular whether or not the discussions meet the standards set out in Chapter 1 for a well-functioning deliberative meeting. Indeed, the anecdotal evidence reported in the press suggests quite the opposite, with members of Congress mostly using town halls to mobilize partisan supporters, and opposing constituents arriving primed for shouting matches with each other and their representative.

Our online deliberative town halls recreated this direct form of representation, but with a better cross section of constituents, who arrived prepared with some background knowledge about the scope and complexity of immigration policy. So our deliberative town halls present an opportunity for us to observe directly how members of Congress interact with their constituents in a setting more conducive to persuasion. In previous chapters, we have shown that the constituents who show up to our sessions tend to be fairly representative of others in the district, and they tend to prepare ahead of time in order to be able to participate in an informed manner. In this chapter, we focus on the third criterion for a deliberative meeting, whether or not the discussion centered on an exchange of reasons that constituents might reasonably find persuasive. That is, we use evidence from our session to evaluate whether the elected representatives take the opportunity to engage in attempts to persuade their constituents on the merits of policies, and if so, whether constituents are receptive to the representatives' arguments.

Below, we begin by sketching the basic criteria for deliberative persuasion. We then present qualitative evidence that representatives, against standard expectations, spent almost all of their time making substantive arguments and attempting to persuade on the merits. Next, we present a more systematic assessment of the discussions using the well-validated Discourse Quality Index (DQI).[1] Our discussions meet or exceed the level of discourse quality found in established deliberative institutions. We follow this analysis up with a discussion of the kinds of rationales offered in the deliberative sessions, and how they align with citizens' views on policy. Finally, having documented that representatives make great efforts to offer compelling arguments, we close by demonstrating that the constituents were indeed persuaded based on these arguments. Thus, both the representatives and the constituents participated in a way that met our third criterion for a well-functioning deliberative institution.

---

[1] Jürg Steiner et al., *Deliberative Politics in Action: Analysing Parliamentary Discourse* (New York: Cambridge University Press, 2004).

THE UNFORCED FORCE OF THE BETTER ARGUMENT

In order to evaluate the merits of the discussion in our sessions, we begin by setting out the basic aspirations for discourse within democratic institutions. The leading idea here is persuasion via "the unforced force of the better argument."[2] Deliberative democrats argue that reasonable attempts at persuasion in public discourse are necessary for democratic legitimacy. While it is always possible to resolve disputes through majority voting, the simple fact of being in a majority itself does not make one's position morally or intellectually compelling. Instead, if parties to a dispute offer reasons for their positions, and in particular, the kinds of reasons that could be accepted by others, then it might be possible for the disputants to find common ground, or short of finding common ground, at least understand the reasonableness of those with whom they disagree. In this way, even those who might ultimately be on the losing side of a majority vote could see the outcome as democratically legitimate.[3]

High quality persuasive discourse has two components, one centering on the kinds of arguments that are made in discussion, and one centering on the participants' receptiveness to those arguments. That is to say, our definition of persuasive discourse involves both the speaker and the listener. First, speakers should offer compelling *rationales* for the positions that they advocate within the discussion. A compelling rationale is one that in principle could be accepted by others who do not already share the speaker's predisposition. For example, an argument based solely on the speaker's own self-interest, such as saying that the policy would make the speaker herself wealthier but with no benefit to others, would not be a rationale that others would likely accept, unless it was accompanied by some special claim of desert. Instead, a compelling rationale is generally one that is stated in a way that appeals to the broader interests of others and perhaps society as a whole.

Second, those who are listening to the arguments should be willing to consider the merits of policy proposals that do not match their initial predispositions and be open to persuasion on the merits of the speaker's arguments. Here, listeners would not meet this expectation if they only participate in the discussion in order to express or confirm their prior beliefs. For example, imagine constituents arriving at a deliberative town hall seeking to participate as die-hard partisans and shout down those who hold different perspectives. As we discuss in the conclusion, there

[2] Jürgen Habermas, *Between Facts and Norms: Contributions to a Discourse Theory of Law and Democracy*, trans. William Rehg (Cambridge, MA: MIT Press, 1996).

[3] Cohen, "Deliberation and Democratic Legitimacy."

certainly is a place for protest and even civil disobedience to create conditions that enable good deliberation. But shouting cannot become the default in a healthy democracy. Instead, citizens generally should be willing to consider alternative viewpoints, recognizing that their views may be mistaken or at least questionable.

When discourse meets these two conditions, it is possible that parties to a discussion can find common ground for policy that is broadly agreeable through a process of *persuasion*. Persuasion occurs when a listener changes an attitude or behavior in response to a speaker's arguments, but only when the listener accepts the speaker's rationale in the absence of coercion.

Many observers would rightfully express a dose of caution, if not skepticism, about the prospects for this kind of rational discourse occurring at our online events, especially when considering how legislators are often portrayed in the media as overwhelmingly strategic and insincere. For example, contrast the aspirations for our sessions with how the media portrayed a set of House Republican field hearings that were being held on the topic of US immigration policy at the same time we conducted our deliberative town halls on the same topic. The *Washington Post,* for example, reported that these field hearings were simply a strategic exercise to work up the Republican base, and stood as "the clearest sign yet that House Republicans have largely given up on passing a broad rewrite of the nation's immigration laws this year."[4]

To the extent that political science has considered the prospects of rational discourse at congressional town halls at all, we can only find another note of caution. In researching *Home Style*, Fenno traveled with members of Congress to their districts to observe directly how they interacted with their constituents. While he sometimes observed representatives explaining their policy positions, he concluded that representatives generally did not offer these explanations in order to persuade constituents on the substantive merits of a policy. Instead, representatives offered these explanations in order to demonstrate their personal qualities in what Fenno refers to as a "presentation of self" – a demonstration that the representative had good intentions for supporting a given policy as a way to gain constituents' trust, if not their agreement. In Fenno's observations, it was relatively rare for representatives to offer explanations in an attempt to persuade their constituents because most of the constituents in attendance either already agreed with them or were not persuadable.[5]

[4] Jonathan Weisman and Shailagh Murray, "GOP Plans Hearings on Issue of Immigrants," *Washington Post,* June 21, 2006, Accessed May 29, 2018. www.washingtonpost.com/wp-dyn/content/article/2006/06/20/AR2006062000926.html.

[5] Fenno, *Home Style: House Members in Their Districts,* 134.

So, both anecdotal evidence from news reporting and the available evidence from the political science literature suggest that we should be cautious in expecting that representatives will meet the first element of our aspirations for rational discourse in our sessions – that the representatives would be willing to offer compelling rationales to their constituents in an attempt to persuade them to support their policy positions, especially to constituents who do not begin the session sharing the representative's own predisposition.

Likewise, many portraits in the news media characterize the citizens who are active in politics as typically motivated by anger, behaving uncivilly and disrespectfully in their participation, polarized as rigid partisans, and remaining closed-minded to alternative views. For example, *Vox* columnist Ezra Klein states, "Perhaps the single most important fact about American politics is this: the people who participate are more ideological and more partisan, as well as angrier and more fearful, than those who don't."[6] And as we discussed in Chapter 1, many commentators are especially concerned that such incivility is only enhanced in an online setting such as ours.[7]

Survey researchers have investigated systematically whether most people are open to new evidence and to persuasion, and their findings support these pessimistic expectations. For example, scholars have developed an extensive survey research literature showing that the mass media have very little power to move public opinion through persuasion,[8] finding either that the public is unresponsive to messages that conflict with their predispositions,[9] or that politicians simply adapt their own messages to fit those predispositions.[10] Combining the anecdotal evidence from the media on how both representatives and citizens typically engage in democratic politics with the scientific evidence on the lack of receptiveness most citizens have to new arguments, it would be reasonable to expect little in the way

---

[6] See Ezra Klein, "The single most important fact about American politics," *Vox*, June 13, 2014, Accessed May 29, 2018. www.vox.com/2014/6/13/5803768/pew-most-important-fact-american-politics.

[7] Ashley A. Anderson et al., "The 'Nasty Effect:' Online Incivility and Risk Perceptions of Emerging Technologies," *Journal of Computer-Mediated Communication* 19, no. 3 (2014): 373–87.

[8] Donald R. Kinder, "Communication and Politics in the Age of Information," in *Oxford Handbook of Political Psychology*, eds. David O. Sears, Leonie Huddy, and Robert Jervis (New York: Oxford University Press, 2003), 357–93; and Benjamin I. Page and Robert Y. Shapiro, *The Rational Public: Fifty Years of Trends in Americans' Policy Preferences* (Chicago: University of Chicago Press, 2010).

[9] Steven E. Finkel, "Reexamining the 'Minimal Effects' Model in Recent Presidential Campaigns," *The Journal of Politics* 55, no. 1 (1993): 1–21.

[10] Robert S. Erikson, Michael B. MacKuen, and James A. Stimson, *The Macro Polity* (Cambridge: Cambridge University Press, 2002).

of rational discourse at our online events. It would seem unlikely that representatives would bother offering compelling rationales and that, even were they to do so, that constituents would be responsive to them.

We expect, however, that the discussion at our deliberative town halls will be different, and more constructive, than the typical town hall for many reasons. First, as we demonstrated in Chapter 3, a fairly representative cross section of constituents showed up to participate in our sessions. As a result, the representatives understood that they would be speaking with constituents who held a variety of perspectives, rather than strong supporters who did not need to be persuaded and implacable opponents who could not be persuaded. Second, as we showed in Chapter 4, the constituents who showed up had an opportunity to become informed about the topic of US immigration policy, and hence the representatives knew that the constituents were better equipped to talk about the policy beyond mere platitudes and soundbites. Third, each session was moderated by a member of the research team, and so suggested that the event was independent of the representative's office. Finally, the exchange was unscripted and free flowing, with the representative responding in her own voice, off-the-cuff, to questions and comments posed by the constituents.

EAVESDROPPING ON DEMOCRACY

In observing these sessions as they were happening, and then later systematically analyzing them, we were struck by the degree to which both constituents and representatives approached the topic with seriousness and substance, treating each other with respect. While civility is a somewhat amorphous concept, we note that our protocol required a screener from the research team to filter out any questions or comments that were "inflammatory, vulgar, or abusive." Remarkably, in the nineteen sessions, with over a thousand questions and comments submitted, the screener never had to invoke that provision – not once. Contrast that with the scenes of incivility at standard town halls, and more generally to the amount of incivility that one typically sees in online settings where participants observe even fewer social constraints than in face-to-face settings.[11]

In response to this serious and civil audience, the representatives responded to constituents' questions and comments with thoughtful, informed, and substantive answers that were clearly aimed at persuasion.

---

[11] Ashley A. Anderson et al., "The 'Nasty Effect': Online Incivility and Risk Perceptions of Emerging Technologies."

Indeed, the representatives did not hold back from openly disagreeing with their constituents, trying instead to persuade them to their views. Take, for example, the argument Congressman Conaway makes in response to a statement from a constituent named Sam who says:

[SAM]: Personally I believe that anyone in this country illegally is a criminal and I don't believe in rewarding lawbreakers. I certainly believe that they should not have any of the benefits that a citizen has. If you must have the guest worker programs, make them for the people that have obtained all the necessary documentation, deport the rest to their home countries.

And then Conaway, a conservative Republican from Texas, responds by disagreeing with Sam's proposal and providing a careful set of rationales for why he disagrees:

[CONAWAY]: Sam, I agree with you that we are a nation of law abiding citizens and it is an affront to our sense of right and wrong to have people here who have broken our laws to come into this country. But from a pragmatic standpoint, I don't believe that deporting 12 million people is something that we're going to start out to do or is realistic to do. If I run a red light, there's a certain penalty. If I rob a bank, there's a certain penalty. I think that you and I together can craft, collectively, we can craft a set of penalties and fines to address those people that the only thing they've done wrong is sneak into this country and stay here illegally.

   If they've broken our laws in some other ways, then of course the full force of the justice system should be applied to them. But we're basically talking about the people who have come into this country and have overstayed their visa or have snuck in to get a job. So let's find what's the right penalty for that group, either a fine or something that satisfies our sense of right and wrong, our sense of paying a debt to society so to speak. But we also have to recognize that these eleven to twelve million people are, for the most part, providing goods and services that you and I use and buy at prices that you and I like to have. And so they are providing a benefit to this economy.

Sam is staking out a strong conservative position on immigration policy, including advocating deportation. Conaway, however, pushed back with a pragmatic argument that deportation is not practical, and also a normative argument that deportation is a penalty that is disproportionate to the crime.

In the same session, Conaway also pushed back in the other direction against a more liberal constituent named Melissa who argued:

[MELISSA]: As one of the most prosperous countries in the world it is important that we do our part to share those blessings with those less fortunate, and allowing increased immigration would afford more people the opportunities that are available in this country.

Conaway replies:

[CONAWAY]: Melissa, thanks for that comment. Much of the rhetoric that surrounds this topic, whether it's the people wanting to talk about border security, or those wanting to talk about immigration and illegal immigration has over the past year gotten very heated and sometimes in some instances has gotten incredibly harsh and mean spirited. This is a concern for all of us. It is an arena in which it is okay for we Americans to operate in our own best interest. We are a country of immigrants. But we are also a country of law abiding citizens. So, somehow we have to craft a good public policy that protects the taxpayers in the United States, but also recognizes that this country is built, has been built by immigrants and that future immigration is going to be very important to the progress of the United States.

My view is to kind of get this thing started, my view is a three-legged stool that we should be working on. First leg is border security. And all that that represents. Second leg would be what we do, or how do we deal with the eleven to twelve million people that are reported to be in this country illegally. And the third leg of the stool would be rational immigration reform, and that refers to the policies that relate to the way we immigrate people into this country. The bureaucracy that provides those services currently is not doing a good job in many of the instances. So I would view border security and immigration to be revolving around those three legs of the stool.

In responding to Melissa, Conaway first laments that much of the discourse surrounding immigration policy is heated and at times harsh, which establishes common ground, but then states his own view that conditions the treatment of current immigrants on enforcement and border security.

Likewise, Congressman Radanovich, a Republican from California's central valley who favors immigration reform, responds to a question from a constituent named Terry by expressing the rationale for his disagreement with her statement. She asks:

[TERRY]: Why do we spend so much on illegal immigrants when we have poverty stricken residents who would love to work but cannot find employment?

[RADANOVICH]: Well, because the United States is a kind and gentle nation. I mean that we are not going to allow anybody, whether they're a citizen or not, to starve on the street. It's just not what we are as Americans. And so, because of the fact these people are here and do need these kind of services, America steps up to the plate. And that is a good thing.

Here, Radanovich is justifying his more liberal approach to immigration policy, relative to the position Terry stakes out, by reference to common American values. At another point, Congressman Radanovich responded to a comment from a constituent named Chuck, who states:

[CHUCK]: I'm of the opinion that we still need to address enforcement first. We've been down this road before and along the line of enforcement got the short end. For now, we need to be sure that enforcement is done and not lost in the shuffle as it was under President Reagan. I work in healthcare, and we're getting killed by the cost of serving illegals.

To which Radanovich replies by explaining that the solutions to the problem of immigration are complex and multifaceted:

[RADANOVICH]:   Thank you, Chuck. You've got an excellent statement. And I will say that enforcing the border is the first and foremost priority because we want to make sure that we protect our borders, I think mainly from terrorists but also from illegals coming into the country. I object to sequencing this because I think that we ought to move forward on a three-pronged approach. Keeping in mind that when Congress passes a law it does not mean it will go into effect 100% the next day. Any one of these initiatives are going to take time. Enforcing the borders will, developing a guest worker program that works, that allows people to come in that will work and go home and not allow bad people in, and this process of getting through the undocumented workers now in this country is going to be daunting. I think all three of them need to be started now. And I think if we do that, we'll have this problem under control a lot quicker than if we wait to enforce the borders first, then develop a guest worker program and then go to getting through this list of undocumented workers. I think we'll get it done sooner if we do all three at once.

In each of these exchanges, the member of Congress not only expresses disagreement with the constituent, but gives specific rationales for why they disagree with the constituent's position. On their face, these are clearly attempts at persuasion within the sessions. Moreover, such substantive attempts at persuasion were the rule rather than the exception. We believe that the level and quality of the discussion were remarkably high as a general matter. To further substantiate this claim beyond our own perceptions, we now turn to a more systematic analysis of the deliberative sessions themselves.

THE QUALITY OF DISCOURSE

To present a more systematic portrayal of the statements from representatives, we extensively coded the transcripts of the sessions. We first developed a set of evaluative "codes" that we can use to classify each of the statements that representatives made at the sessions. We then had a team of research assistants (diverse in their ideological and partisan commitments) code the arguments and statements that representatives make. We based our coding scheme on the well-validated DQI,[12] supplemented by extra coding items of our own, designed to address a few lacunae in the DQI.

The DQI's *level of justification* coding category captures whether a speaker provides a justification for her claims or policy positions. An argument is coded as having no justification if the speaker takes a policy position without giving a reason or justification. An argument is coded as having an inferior justification if the speaker offers a reason Y for policy position X, but no linkage is made between X and Y. The inference is incomplete. Arguments are also labeled as inferior if a conclusion is merely supported with illustrations or analogies. We code an argument as having qualified justification if the speaker posits a linkage as to

[12] Steiner et al., *Deliberative Politics in Action: Analysing Parliamentary Discourse*. For a broader philosophical discussion of deliberative quality, see Susan Dorr Goold et al., "What Is Good Public Deliberation?," *The Hastings Center Report* 42, no. 2 (2012): 24–6; and André Bächtiger et al., "Disentangling Diversity in Deliberative Democracy: Competing Theories, Their Blind Spots and Complementarities," *The Journal of Political Philosophy* 18, no. 1 (2010): 32–63.

why reason Y should encourage or detract support from policy position X. A single such complete inference qualifies for this code. Finally, an argument is coded as having a sophisticated justification if the speaker provides at least two complete justifications: either two complete justifications for the same argument, or complete justifications for two different arguments.

Overall, across all nineteen sessions, we found an average of 19 percent of responses that the representatives make to their constituents' questions and comments to have no or inferior justifications, 34 percent to have qualified justifications, and 47 percent to have sophisticated justifications. This distribution is quite high relative to other venues in the DQI literature. Indeed, they exceed the findings on several other prominent sites of deliberation using these same coding measures: parliamentary debate in the United States, Switzerland, Germany, and the United Kingdom[13] as well as the *Europolis*, perhaps the biggest and most ambitious deliberative forum ever fielded.[14] Far from "dumbing it down," members of Congress in our events provided higher levels of justification than they typically do in their floor speeches or their peers do in parliaments around the world.

Moreover, the evidence backing the justifications was also strong. While representatives frequently appealed to anecdotes, they appealed to public facts at almost triple the rate of anecdotes. Across all of the sessions, in only four instances, out of hundreds, did a representative appeal to something that was factually inaccurate, whereas there were twenty-one instances of representatives admitting that they did not know some salient piece of information in the discussions (whereupon they usually offered to find out if the constituent followed up with their office). In addition, rather than demonizing the other side, remarkably, *in every session*, the representative acknowledged that there was a legitimate other

---

[13] André Bächtiger and John Parkinson, *Mapping and Measuring Deliberation: Micro and macro knowledge of deliberative quality, dynamics and contexts* (Oxford: Oxford University Press, 2018); see also André Bächtiger and Marina Lindell, "'Benchmarking' Deliberative Quality across Sites," *Political Communication* 26 (Fall 2016): 1–2.

[14] James S. Fishkin, Robert C. Luskin, and Alice Siu, "Europolis and the European Public Sphere: Empirical Explorations of a Counterfactual Ideal," *European Union Politics* 15, no. 3 (May 16, 2014): 328–51; Lauren B. Cheatham and Zakary L. Tormala, "The Curvilinear Relationship Between Attitude Certainty and Attitudinal Advocacy," *Personality and Social Psychology Bulletin* 43, no. 1 (2017): 3–16; Marlène Gerber et al., "Deliberative abilities and influence in a transnational Deliberative Poll (EuroPolis)," *British Journal of Political Science* (2016): 1–26; and Marlène Gerber et al., "Deliberative and non-deliberative persuasion: Mechanisms of opinion formation in EuroPolis," *European Union Politics* 15, no. 3 (2014): 410–29.

side to the issue, and in over two-thirds they explicitly extolled the merits of a counterargument to his or her own position.

There were occasionally expressions of disrespect (in eight sessions), though every one of them was directed at the *arguments* of opponents (e.g., "I think that proposal is crazy."), rather than the opponents themselves or the people involved in the policy question (i.e., there were no examples such as "Many of these immigrants were rapists or murderers."). The contrast with many other forms of public discourse is quite striking.

The DQI, however, only measures the formal properties of arguments. That is to say, it does not attempt to assess the substantive quality of arguments, or the sincerity with which they are offered. So a formally correct set of arguments as measured by the DQI may nonetheless be utterly unpersuasive if its content is not compelling. For example, consider the debate over the notorious Alaskan "bridge to nowhere" in the US Senate.[15] Arguments in favor of the bridge, though formally of high quality, appeared as pure pork-barrel politics to almost all disinterested observers (e.g., the bridge connected to uninhabited land on one end). The main deliberative theory that we rely on requires that speakers also offer substantively compelling arguments, and that they do so sincerely.[16]

So we supplemented the DQI with "substantive quality" and "sincerity" codes. Although we employed an ideologically diverse set of coders, perhaps surprisingly, we achieved reasonable levels of inter-coder reliability (agreement around 80 percent). That is, we could get both conservative and liberal coders to agree most of the time on whether an argument was substantively sound, and whether the representatives appeared to be offering them sincerely or insincerely. This finding may be surprising, but research in social psychology suggests that most of us are fairly good at assessing a speaker's sincerity, even it is only via a gestalt impression.[17]

We coded the sessions for substantive quality at the *response level*, i.e., for the entire response given by a member of Congress in response to a constituent's question. These codes were implemented by five different coders where two of the coders self-identify as politically conservative and three self-identify as politically liberal. The coders evaluated

[15] Michael A. Neblo, "Family Disputes: Diversity in Defining and Measuring Deliberation," *Swiss Political Science Review* 13, no. 4 (December 1, 2007): 527–57.

[16] Habermas, *Between Facts and Norms: Contributions to a Discourse Theory of Law and Democracy.*

[17] Bella M. DePaulo et al., "Cues to Deception," *Psychological Bulletin* 129, no. 1 (January 2003): 74–118. For further details on our coding, see Michael A. Neblo et al., "Measuring sincerity and the substantive content of arguments in deliberation," *Program on Networked Governance* (Working Paper PNG No. PNG08–001).

the representatives' arguments along a spectrum of quality, with coding labels ranging from repellant (–1), to uncompelling (0), to compelling (1), to convincing (2). In a small number of cases (3 percent) the coders actually found the argument perverse – i.e., reinforcing the opposite view from what the speaker intended. In a quarter of the cases, they found the argument uncompelling and gave it little credence. But in the great majority of cases they found the arguments either compelling (42 percent) or convincing (30 percent). They also rated the representatives as apparently sincere, with slightly less than 10 percent of the statements coming off as insincerely offered. These results track comments from the constituents themselves who very occasionally opined things like "I feel it was typical government smoke," but as we detail in Chapter 6, on the whole expressed strongly positive attitudes toward the representatives' candor.

PERSUASION IN THE DELIBERATIVE TOWN HALLS

We have thus far presented considerable evidence that the representatives who participated in our deliberative town halls made extensive attempts at persuading their constituents using substantive and rational discourse. The next question, then, is if those statements had any effect on constituents, or if those carefully crafted arguments simply fell on deaf ears, as many steeped in the public opinion survey research literature would expect.

Indeed, despite the centrality of persuasion in democracy, there is remarkably little evidence to show whether or not unmediated appeals from political actors have any persuasive effects on constituents. The biggest barriers to studying such persuasion are methodological; it is difficult to conduct systematic research on ordinary town halls because researchers cannot generally randomize citizens to attend or refrain from attending. Researchers have studied hypothetical elite-mass interactions in a laboratory setting.[18] But we do not know whether these laboratory findings track real encounters between representatives and constituents in the actual practice of democracy. Indeed, as we saw in Chapter 3, it is possible for hypothetical scenarios to reverse their findings relative to what we observe when those scenarios play out in practice.

We tailored our experiments to observe how representatives interact with their constituents on policy questions, and to test whether persuasion

---

[18] Milton Lodge, Kathleen M. McGraw, and Patrick Stroh, "An Impression-Driven Model of Candidate Evaluation," *The American Political Science Review* 83, no. 2 (June 1989): 399–419; and Dennis Chong and James N. Druckman, "Framing Public Opinion in Competitive Democracies," *The American Political Science Review* 101, no. 4 (November 2007): 637–55.

occurs within representative-constituent interactions. Our study is the first systematic opportunity to evaluate the effects of representative-constituent interactions on constituents' attitudes. Furthermore, our platform affords a novel opportunity for constituents to engage in an informed, constructive discussion with their member of Congress.

We focus here on substantive persuasion, which centers on changes in constituents' attitudes about what is desirable public policy. This sort of persuasion is the ordinary meaning of the word and, as we describe above, engenders a kind of rational conviction that is necessary to ensure democratic legitimacy.

To test the effects of representatives' appeals on constituents, we compare the change in participants' responses to questions asking their position on several immigration policies, from a baseline survey, administered about two weeks prior to the session, to a follow up survey, which we administered about one week after the session.[19] Keep in mind that we administered the same surveys to both those who participated in the deliberative town hall session and those who did not, so we can compare differences across these two groups. The full study has two types of groups to which we can compare our deliberators: *true controls* who received no reading materials and the *information only controls* who received reading materials, but did not participate in a session. In this part of our analysis we will only compare the deliberative participants to the information only controls. We chose this comparison because both sets of respondents had an opportunity to read the same background material. Hence it enables us to test for the effect of the session itself – that is, it is a harder test of our present claims.

We test for substantive persuasion by examining whether the participants' attitudes regarding a path to citizenship for undocumented immigrants moved toward their representative's views. Representatives and constituents brought up the path to citizenship issue regularly in the sessions; they used the words "amnesty" and "citizenship" over 150 times. And constituents moved sharply toward their representative's position.

To test whether this pattern is due to persuasion or some other extraneous cause, we conducted a "placebo test" by examining whether constituents moved toward their representative on a topic that did not come up in the sessions – in this case, whether to change the number of *legal*

---

[19] This section on persuasion in the deliberative town halls is based on the article William Minozzi et al., "Field Experiment Evidence of Substantive, Attributional, and Behavioral Persuasion by Members of Congress in Online Town Halls," *Proceedings of the National Academy of Sciences,* 2015. We gratefully acknowledge the contributions of William Minozzi who was the lead author on the paper.

immigrants allowed to enter the country. The discussants barely mentioned this topic in the sessions, and indeed we found no evidence that constituents who participated in the sessions moved toward their representative on this question.

Perhaps most surprisingly, though, we found similar patterns of persuasion among constituents from both political parties. That is, Democratic representatives were equally effective in persuading Republican and Democratic constituents, and Republican representatives persuading Democratic and Republican constituents. This finding is remarkable given the level of polarization in today's politics, and underscores our assertion that the constituents in our sessions were open to listening to opinions different from their own.

Moreover, we have good, if circumstantial, evidence that these changes were underwritten by facts and reasons. For example, citizens in the deliberative group, but not the two control conditions, tended to move their policy position in tandem with their issue specific knowledge gains. That is, in the deliberative condition people who learned the most about the issues were also the ones who changed their minds about the issues.

REPRESENTATION AS TWO-WAY CONVERSATION

The representatives in our study offered reasons for their positions, and engaged constituents in a way that was respectful of their views while also articulating disagreements. In turn, the constituents on the whole found the representatives to be persuasive. For representation to be effective, however, not only should representatives clarify their views in a process of ongoing deliberative accountability, but also representatives need to be open to understanding the views of their constituents via ongoing republican consultation. Effective representation, that is, must be a two-way street.

We should be clear that our study was primarily designed to understand the impact of deliberative town hall participation on constituents, and as a result the evidence that we have for the impact of the deliberative town halls on the representative is only suggestive. The best evidence that we have that the representatives used the sessions as a vehicle for republican consultation comes from the closing remarks that they made at the conclusion of their session. Here, several representatives themselves state that they found the sessions valuable to understand constituents' views. For example, Congresswoman Eshoo (D, CA-14) stated,

I always learn from what my constituents say to me. There are several things that were expressed to me this evening that really were not, have not been brought into focus for me. So I appreciate it.

Likewise, Congressman Weldon (R, FL-15) states,

This has been a great session; I've really enjoyed it. They've been great questions. I hope it was very informative to those who were on the program. And I'm certainly looking forward to getting further feedback that you may have. You can call my congressional office or write to me and, you can also e-mail me. I'd love to hear from you.

And Congressman Price (D, NC-4),

Well, these are good questions and it's clear that they represent diverse points of views and they represent people searching their own consciousness and minds for an answer to these difficult questions ... There's so much, so much overheated rhetoric about this issue and so much contention, that it's really refreshing for me to see people grappling with these real questions in a serious and civil thing. So I really appreciate this and I think that there's not a question that was posed that was not a legitimate question, and one that needs to be answered as we move ahead to try to resolve this issue. So I appreciate the quality and the tenor of the questions.

Since the representatives are self-reporting these reactions, one cannot take these comments as a decisive demonstration of the impact of the sessions on the representatives as a vehicle for republican consultation. The statements are, however, strongly suggestive that the representatives valued the sessions, valued the constituents' input, and found the events to be of high value to them as effective representatives.

CONCLUSION

Contrary to the expectations of many political observers, we demonstrate that the representatives who participated in our events made reasoned attempts to persuade their constituents about the merits of their positions. While the question remains whether or not persuasion occurs in face-to-face town halls, we can say definitively that representatives do persuade in our online deliberative town halls, demonstrating that indeed, representatives make arguments to their constituents that appeal to reasons and can be accepted by others. Moreover, constituents listen to these arguments and consider them seriously enough to change their opinion. Thus, we find that our sessions met the third criterion of a successful deliberative event, that they generally featured rational and reasoned argumentation.

It remains to be seen, however, whether such persuasive interaction affects the representative relationship itself – that is, whether directly representative democracy can engender warranted trust, which is our fourth criterion.

6

Representative Connections

Sometimes I wonder whether the job is to find out what people want and do it, or do what you want and hope people want it. In the end, though, when I do what I want, I'm so much like them that they'll agree with me. For that reason, I think it's better not to come home and make speeches, but rather to come home ... and talk to people to keep up with the rhythms of what they are saying.

—Congresswoman Zoe Lofgren[1]

As Congresswoman Lofgren reflects on the nature of her job as an elected representative in the quote above, she implicitly invokes the classic distinction between a delegate (find out what people want and do it) and a trustee (do what you think best and hope people want it).[2] But then she steps outside of that framework and argues that her judgment has been tutored in such a way that simply exercising it will yield results that align with her constituents' wishes. In doing so, she is (again implicitly) articulating a more nuanced theory of representation called the "gyroscopic" model.[3] *Gyroscopic* is meant to indicate that the representative can maintain her orientation vis-a-vis her constituents on new issues by referencing her own pre-aligned values, in that a gyroscope constantly reorients itself into an upright position, even when buffeted by external forces. On this model, then, a representative can often behave like a trustee on

---

[1] Richard F. Fenno, *The Challenge of Congressional Representation* (Cambridge, MA: Harvard University Press, 2013).

[2] Pitkin, *The Concept of Representation.*

[3] Jane Mansbridge, "Clarifying the Concept of Representation," *The American Political Science Review* 105, no. 3 (August 2011): 621–30.

a given issue but produce the effects of a delegate if she "thinks, reasons, and feels" like her constituents.[4] Notice, though, that Rep. Lofgren does not just assume that her ability to do so is some innate and permanent trait. Rather she must cultivate it by staying attuned to how her constituents are thinking, for example, as she did through participating in our experiment.[5]

Fenno anticipated something related to the gyroscopic model when he argued that members of Congress attend to presentation of self in order to gain their constituents' trust.[6] One might say that representatives go to great lengths to convince their constituents that the representatives have well calibrated gyroscopes. But Fenno missed two important elements of the model. First, he did not take account of the way that elected officials might be open to mutual influence – "to keep up with the rhythms of what [their constituents] are saying" in order to *actually* calibrate their gyroscopes. To Fenno, presentation of self is something that the representative does, but it is only a one-way street. On Lofgren's account, interacting with constituents helps to keep the metaphorical gyroscope spinning by engaging in two-way communication.

Second, Fenno did not appreciate the extent to which engaging constituents in republican consultation and deliberative accountability can itself serve as an effective presentation of self. As we show below, citizens gave the representatives enormous credit for reaching out to consult them in the first place, as well as for engaging with them substantively. Contrary to their apparent behavior in standard town halls, representatives focused almost entirely on reasoned persuasion when they saw that they were interacting with persuadable constituents. The constituents rewarded them with increased trust and approval, creating more space for them to exercise their judgment without having to engage in intensive consultation on every issue. A little bit of directly representative

---

[4] For a similar argument applied to politically independent judges, see Kevin M. Esterling, "Public outreach: The cornerstone of judicial independence," *Judicature* 82, no. 3 (1998): 112.

[5] Scholars arguing for the gyroscopic model presume that it emerges from evolutionary pressures – elected officials who do not have well-functioning gyroscopes lose reelection. There may be truth in this claim, but here we focus on how elected officials *cultivate* their gyroscopic alignment. In addition, on our account "producing the effects of a delegate" would mean mirroring the latent or deliberative opinion of constituents, rather than raw opinion.

[6] Morris P. Fiorina and David W. Rohde, eds. *Home Style and Washington Work: Studies of Congressional Politics* (Ann Arbor: University of Michigan Press, 1991), 7.

democracy can go a long way by enabling representatives to do well by doing right.

Cultivating trust is crucial for the deliberative system because most citizens cannot and should not quit their day jobs to deliberate about every issue. Representative democracy needs citizens to develop warranted trust in their elected officials. That is to say, citizens need to have good reasons to believe that their representative's gyroscope is working properly. In turn, as Fenno argues, elected officials have incentives to engage in practices that foster this warranted trust, not only because trust is more likely to attract votes in a reelection campaign, but also because trust enables representatives to pursue good policies even when they are apparently inconsistent with constituents hastily considered opinions.

Well-functioning deliberative events, then, should spill beyond their local concerns to foster trust within the representative relationship. Our experiments were designed to test whether opportunities for republican consultation and deliberative accountability produced such desiderata. Below we show that they emphatically did. Representatives increased their constituents' trust, approval, and likelihood of voting for them. Constituents who participated in the sessions increased their sense of political efficacy, were extremely enthusiastic about the events, expressed a desire to do more of them, and believed their participation was important for democracy. In this way, our deliberative town halls created a virtuous circle that was beneficial to representatives and constituents alike. Thus, they met our fourth criterion for a well-structured deliberative event.

CITIZENS' ASSESSMENT OF DIRECT REPRESENTATION

After each representative completed her session with constituents, we logged the representative out of the deliberative town hall, and we then transferred the constituents into a text-based chat room where we invited them to type comments and interact with each other about the session. The chats followed a remarkably consistent pattern: the constituents began by discussing their general views of the session and the performance of the representative. Then, after ten to thirty comments, one of the constituents would offer a substantive view on immigration which triggered a discussion of the issue for the remainder of the chat.

A simple count of the tone of the opening comments in the chat sessions found about 14 percent were negative and 86 percent were positive about the quality of the event. The only negative statements about the design of the online deliberative town halls themselves centered on time constraints – constituents did not want the sessions to end so soon, indicating that they thought what they were doing was important and enjoyable. A typical comment along these lines was:

Definitely not enough time to address all comments. Would be nice to have him answer all of the questions posed to him.

Even with enough time, of course, one cannot please all the people all the time, and it is a time-honored tradition in American politics to criticize politicians. Examples of such criticism include:

I truly thought it was more of a soap box for Congressman [X] than real discussion on immigration.
I feel they were political answers. In other words, he said nothing about fixing the problem.
She's a Democrat and mostly follows the party line.
I'm not sure her facts are correct. For example, I know attorneys who say many illegal immigrants are not deported after being convicted of crimes.

It is important to keep in mind, however, that the relative number of negative comments was very low – about one for every *six* positive comments. As a general matter, participants were extremely positive about the sessions. On the follow up survey, a large majority of participants reported that they found the sessions to be helpful and informative (78 percent). Virtually all participants (95 percent) agreed that this kind of deliberative interaction between constituents and representatives is very valuable for our democracy, and would like to participate in a similar session in the future (97 percent). Many constituent comments in the chat room echoed the positive sentiments found in the survey responses:

This was a great forum. It actually made me feel like I had a voice in government.
I believe we are experiencing the one way our elected representatives can hear our voice and do what we want.
That he is having this dialogue online is a great thing, and I would like to see much more of this, with all senators and congressmen.
I don't agree with everything he said, but it was good to get feedback from someone like him who is supposed to be working for us.
I am glad that he took the time to discuss with us, and with the internet more of these discussions should take place with our local officials.

Given such comments, it should come as no surprise that participating in the sessions made constituents much more likely to describe their representative as "accessible."[7] Yet it is still an open question whether the forums directly enhanced constituents' *individual* sense of being effective in the political system. On the follow up survey, everyone in the study was asked whether they agreed with the statement:

I don't think public officials care much what people like me think.

The question is a measure of how much an individual thinks that her voice matters in the political system ("external efficacy"). In comparison to the constituents who only read the background materials, those who participated in the deliberative town hall increased their external efficacy by 8 percent. That is to say, participants increased their belief that the political system will be responsive to their concerns when the time comes for them to express those concerns.[8]

WHY CONSTITUENTS EVALUATE DIRECT REPRESENTATION SO POSITIVELY

Constituents evaluated the sessions positively for many reasons. In particular, though, they focused on the representatives relinquishing control of the conversation to neutral moderators, and found the unscripted exchanges that resulted authentic and constructive. The elected officials knew that they were interacting with an unusually representative cross-section of their constituents who had been provided background materials on immigration policy. But they did not know the questions that the constituents would ask. The sessions required representatives to offer responses in real time, based on their views, deemphasizing the crafted talk of consultants, party leadership, and staffers. The constituents sensed this and liked it a lot.

---

[7] The intent-to-treat coefficient was highly significant, and indicated a 19 percent increase in such ascriptions, with the as-treated change almost double.

[8] Esterling, Neblo, and Lazer, "Estimating treatment effects in the presence of noncompliance and nonresponse: The generalized endogenous treatment model." There was no corresponding increase in participants' sense of "internal efficacy" – the belief that they have important ideas that those in government need to listen to. We conjecture that this null effect may result from gains from those who were overly humble cancelling out declines in those who may have thought that policy was simpler than they originally thought.

Representatives prefer to control the message coming from their offices carefully. But by giving up tight control, paradoxically, the representatives were more able to persuade. Many citizens default to a posture of distrust and skepticism vis-à-vis politicians. However, the constituents in our sessions perceived that their representatives were being candid because of the spontaneity and third-party moderation of our session. For many constituents, these features changed their posture toward the interaction. The sessions felt more like a serious conversation than an infomercial. Constituents made statements to this effect over and over. For example,

I thought he really tried to address the issues we were bringing up instead of steering the conversation in any particular direction, which was cool.
It was nice to see that he had some detailed answers to our questions, and not just skip over them or give us a one word answer.
Very candid.
He seemed to really listen and think about our questions. No sound bites.
He never avoided a question.

Remarkably, this last statement is true of every representative in every session – not once did a representative avoid answering a question. In a few cases, the representative admitted ignorance regarding some factual matter (itself remarkable), but in each of those cases promised to get back to the constituent with the answer. Though we have no precise bases of comparison, such behavior seems to contrast notably with the way politicians often seem to deflect questions in debates, press conferences, and interviews.

Most constituents also valued the sessions because they perceived that they were able to participate on a basis of equality. Scholars have expressed concern that deliberation might reproduce and even magnify inequalities that exist in society more broadly. For example, research suggests that women, racial and ethnic minorities, the less educated and the poor, sometimes either self-censor or are shut out of deliberation.[9] In our deliberative town halls, however, we find broad and equal participation across such subgroups. We examined several measures of participation and found that in both the sessions as well as the chats, citizens participated on a remarkably equal and inclusive basis. For example, when comparing men to women, or highly educated to less educated, or older

---

[9] Sanders, "Against Deliberation"; and Tali Mendelberg and John Oleske, "Race and Public Deliberation," *Political Communication* 17, no. 2 (2000): 169–91.

to younger, or white to nonwhite participants, we found no statistically significant difference in the number of questions asked or the number of words in the response from the representative.[10] The design of the events likely encouraged such equality. For example, the online format of the events deemphasized cues about social status, and prioritizing questions from people who had not already posed questions encouraged even participation. Unequal participation, then, is not an intrinsic feature of deliberation, but can be mitigated with care in designing its features.

In addition to these objective measures, we administered a brief survey to participants at the conclusion of the session asking them about their participation, their attitudes toward the session, and the platform itself. A large majority (72 percent) reported that they were able to express their views and concerns, and there were no significant differences by race, education or income. On gender there was a difference, but it was women who were (16 percent) *more* likely to strongly agree that they could express their views.

We asked the sixty-four participants (18 percent) who reported they were unable to express their views to let us know why. The great majority, fifty-three of the sixty-four (83 percent), explained that the sessions ended too soon and they could not express their views adequately simply due to time constraints. This actually suggests that they valued the sessions and wished that they could go longer.

GETTING TO KNOW YOU

Only 35 percent of Americans can identify the name and party of their member of the House of Representatives.[11] A substantial majority of constituents, then, do not have any meaningful attitudes about their representative. Given the degree of polarization in contemporary politics, one might wonder whether representatives would do better to let well enough alone. As the great sociologist Paul Lazarsfeld once quipped, however, "In politics, familiarity doesn't breed contempt. It breeds votes."[12] Our findings strongly support Lazarsfeld's maxim, and, indeed, elaborate on

[10] We report these results in Ryan Kennedy et al., "Gender, Deliberation and (Equal?) Voice: Evidence from Online Town Halls," Midwest Political Science Association, 2015.

[11] See "Americans Down on Congress, OK With Own Representative," Gallup, May 9, 2013, Accessed May 29, 2018. www.gallup.com/poll/162362/americans-down-congress-own-representative.aspx.

[12] "Paul Lazarsfeld," Wikiquote, Accessed May 29, 2018. https://en.wikiquote.org/wiki/Paul_Lazarsfeld.

it: direct representation breeds familiarity; familiarity breeds positive attributions about the representative; those attributions breed trust; and trust breeds votes.

We included a set of survey questions designed to evaluate the attributes that Fenno argued were crucial to representatives' presentation of self. It should come as no surprise that citizens who participated in the sessions became more familiar with their representative than the control groups, though it is worth affirming that they did. As a result, participants who attended the deliberative town halls were much more likely to offer attributions about their representatives rather than responding "Don't Know." And those attributions were markedly more positive for participants in the sessions.[13] Participants were significantly more likely than those in the information only condition to say that their representative was: Honest (+17 percent), Fair (+14 percent), Hardworking (+12 percent), Knowledgeable (+9 percent), Qualified (+15 percent), and Understands People Like Me (+11 percent). Moreover, these gains are, statistically speaking, very conservative estimates.[14]

If we think back to the gyroscopic model of representation, these attributes are exactly the characteristics that representatives would actually need for their gyroscopes to work well – i.e., to align with what their constituents would want were they able to deliberate carefully about all the issues. Put another way, if my representative understands people like me, while also being honest, fair, hardworking, knowledgeable and qualified, I have very good reason to believe that she will make good decisions by my lights. These are the very perceptions that Fenno shows representatives work the hardest to cultivate. Many constituent comments conveyed such positive attributions, for example that the representatives were knowledgeable, honest, and hardworking:

I think he was very knowledgeable on most issues. What he didn't know he would be researching.

---

[13] Kevin M. Esterling et al., "The Role of Familiarity in Democratic Representation: A Field Experiment on Constituent Attitudes toward Members of Congress," American Political Science Association Annual Meeting, 2015.

[14] These are "intent-to-treat" estimates. The "as-treated" estimates were almost double on average. Intent-to-treat analyses group by the random assignment, whether or not citizens actually participated in the sessions. As-treated group by the actual participation. The trade-off between them is related to type I and II error. The latter can go wrong if compliance with the treatment is correlated with some trait that can affect the outcomes. The former typically underestimate genuine treatment effects. See the methods appendix for more detail.

He's really surprisingly honest and direct. I think more highly of him than before I did this.

I think she had a lot of good facts to support her opinions.

He wasn't afraid to say that he didn't have all the answers rather than just coming up with something on the spot that might not be realistic.

I thought he was very informative. He pointed out a few things that I wasn't aware of.

I think the Congresswoman handled herself well considering the broad scope of the questions.

The man is intelligent and trying to bring up information that we haven't necessarily thought about, due to our own prejudices. Very good answers, he was very thorough.

I think it says something about him just given the fact he was on this forum.

These were open-ended comments, so constituents spontaneously offered such positive attributions (six times more often than negative attributions). Thus, by engaging both supporters and opponents, representatives were able to enhance the esteem of their constituents on qualities that are central for effective representation.

TRUST, APPROVAL, AND VOTING

Legislators are obliged to further their constituents' interests, but fulfilling that obligation may lead them to depart from their constituents' uninformed, off-the-cuff policy preferences. However, if the legislator departs from what her constituents (perhaps wrongly) *think* is in their interests too often, then she is likely to suffer electoral penalties. When constituents trust representatives to do what is right, however, the representatives can pursue their roles as deliberative representatives more effectively. In many ways then, trust is the key attribute that representatives seek.[15] Being thought honest, hardworking, and knowledgeable is largely instrumental to building trust. Given the robust increases on those antecedent attributions, it should not be surprising that participating in our sessions also increased constituents' trust in their representatives substantially, by 12 percent on average. And perhaps more surprising, the results were slightly *stronger* for constituents who did not share their representative's partisanship.[16]

[15] William T. Bianco, *Trust: Representatives and Constituents* (Ann Arbor: University of Michigan Press, 1994); and Robert J. Boeckmann and Tom R. Tyler, "Trust, respect, and the psychology of political engagement," *Journal of Applied Social Psychology* 32, no. 10 (2002): 2067–88.

[16] These effects, as well as those below, used instrumental-variables regression to estimate the complier average causal effect (CACE).

Increasing trust should create space for representatives to exercise more independence in their judgments without suffering electoral punishment. Obviously, elected officials have a strong interest in their own reelection, so the goal of institutional design is to encourage representatives to do well by doing right – that is, to *earn* their constituents' trust and support through engaging with them constructively and substantively. If directly representative democrats aspire to realistic reform, they need to show that the practices they recommend will help representatives retain their jobs. To test for such an electoral connection, we included questions on the follow up survey asking about approval of the representative and constituents' intent to vote for him or her. Then on the post-election survey we asked whether in fact they voted for the representative.

Relative to constituents who only received background materials, those who participated in our deliberative town hall sessions were 8 percent more likely to approve of their representative, and 14 percent more likely to say that they intended to vote for him or her. Most importantly, participants were 10 percent more likely to actually vote for their representative in the November elections.[17] This voting result is both scientifically and politically striking. It is scientifically striking because, unlike many lab experiments, the causal effect of participating persisted a full four months after the session. It is politically striking because a 10 percent vote swing is enormously consequential in the context of electoral politics,[18] especially in our age of increasing partisan polarization. Given such polarization it is especially remarkable that these increases held for participants who were of the same *and* of the opposing party of the representative, and doubly so given that the diversity of participants meant that it was impossible for representatives to cater to a homogeneous audience.

---

[17] These results also were originally reported in Minozzi et al., *Proceedings of the National Academy of Sciences*. For a more descriptive approach, see also David Lazer, M. Neblo, K. Esterling, and K. Goldschmidt, "Online Town Hall Meetings–Exploring Democracy in the 21st Century," (Washington DC: Congressional Management Foundation, 2009).

[18] Indeed, one might worry that such effects could increase the already considerable advantages of incumbency too much. We are less concerned about this potential problem: (1) because representatives would be doing well by doing right – i.e., it would be an advantage for those who behave in ways that are more congruent with good government; and (2) on a larger scale, we could even imagine a commission on deliberative town-halls (like the one on debates) which could provide moderators, choose topics, and curate background materials. In proximity to elections such a commission might also incorporate challengers to address this issue.

Finally, we found some tentative, but very intriguing, evidence that all of these attributional and electoral effects are likely to persist even farther into the future. We included a set of questions about emotional reactions to the representatives on the post-election survey. The questions fall into three clusters corresponding to what psychologists call the "disposition" system (e.g., enthusiasm), the "surveillance" system (e.g., anxiety), and the "aversion" system (e.g., hatred).[19] The disposition system regulates habits – if it is activated, we reinforce our tendency to stick with what has been working for us. The surveillance system monitors the environment for new opportunities and threats. If it is activated we tend to be open to gathering new information and changing our minds. The aversion system is basically fight or flight. If it is activated we prepare for conflict. Participation in the deliberative sessions activated citizens' disposition system at higher rates, but had little effect on their surveillance or aversion systems. Activating constituents' disposition systems bodes well for building a habit of trusting and voting for the representatives over the long term. Representatives can do well by doing right not only in the short term, but over the long run as well.

To the extent that engaging in directly representative democracy increases representatives' own career goals of reelection, and building trust and esteem in their work as politicians, representatives should have positive incentives to pursue such opportunities actively. In turn, as constituents gain experience engaging in direct representation, they likely would be willing to reinvest the kind of trust and legitimacy in democratic politics that appears to be on the wane in contemporary mass democracy. Indeed, we observed a moderate increase in *general* political trust among constituents as a result of participating in a single session.[20]

The key, however, is to convince representatives to relinquish control of the discussion and to engage equally with the full array of perspectives among constituents in their district. The representatives who participated in our sessions most certainly saw the value of buying into the directly representative paradigm. For example, in his closing remarks, offered spontaneously and off-the-cuff, Congressman Conaway (R, TX-11) articulated well the goals of directly representative democracy as constructive, two-way communication:

---

[19] George E. Marcus, W. Russell Neuman, and Michael MacKuen, *Affective intelligence and political judgment* (Chicago: University of Chicago Press, 2000).

[20] The ITT estimate was 3 percent though statistically non-significant, while the naive estimate was 7 percent and significant.

Let me thank everybody who has taken time out this afternoon to participate in this different way, or new way of helping members of Congress communicate with their constituents. We are, you know, constantly experimenting and trying to find new ways to communicate with constituents because I believe that when people have as many facts as they can about a particular subject then they generally make much better decisions as to what their personal position is. I also think it's important that you as constituents know or at least get some insight into how I make decisions, how I approach problems, how I come to conclusions and that because that's really at the end of the day what you elect me to do. We can't consult with each other on every single vote that I take. But you need to have some comfort in the way that I approach my job ... and this medium gives us a little bit of a chance to talk on something other than thirty second sound bites to help me communicate with you. So I appreciate each one of you that have participated in this afternoon's events.

Clearly, Congressman Conaway shares our belief that informed, constructive two-way communication enables warranted trust in the elected official as a legitimate representative of constituents' interests.

CONCLUSION

Directly representative democracy seeks to transcend the dichotomy between representatives as delegates and trustees. Rather than engaging in a tug-of-war over the proper level of discretion that representatives should have, direct representation opens up the possibility of lessening the tension between the two. If republican consultation and deliberative accountability are working well, then elected representatives and their constituents have more capacity to work through policy problems *together*, rather than representatives either simply taking marching orders or issuing dicta. Moreover, directly representative practices can initiate a virtuous cycle wherein such interaction itself provides the bases of warranted trust in representatives, further lessening the tension, and advancing the legislators' own career interests.

The gyroscopic model of representation captures part of this dynamic. That said, it is not a substitute for directly representative democracy. A variant of the model that attends to the need to *cultivate* gyroscopic sensitivity through republican consultation, however, can play a powerful role in making the deliberative system work well. Direct representation enhances the positive attributions that underwrite trust. Paradoxically, a moderate amount of good quality direct representation lessens the need for constant monitoring. And from the representatives' point of view, trust fosters both room to pursue policy goals and votes to support reelection. Thus, if directly representative institutions can scale up to a critical threshold, they hold out the possibility of setting off a cycle that materially alters the representative relationship.

7

Scaling Up and Scaling Out

I know we love jargon and buzz-words but "retail politics?" What's next: wholesale, discount, or closeout politics?

—DeAmo Murphy

What we shall call opinion leadership, if we may call it leadership at all, is leadership at its simplest: it is casually exercised, sometimes unwitting and unbeknown, within the smallest grouping of friends, family members, and neighbors.

—Katz and Lazarsfeld[1]

So far we have presented directly representative democracy as a form of "retail" politics. Murphy pokes fun at the term, but we find it – and even the other metaphors – surprisingly apt.[2] The sessions with the members of the House of Representatives were relatively small. Moreover, the two-way communication within direct representation seems intrinsically retail, in contrast to the "wholesale" politics communicated via the mass media. On the face of it, then, there are reasons to be skeptical that online town halls could have much of an impact on the broader deliberative system. Simple math suggests that the potential of 535 members of Congress, reaching out to thirty or so people at a time will, in the end, reach a tiny fraction of over 200 million potential voters.

---

[1] DeAmo Murphy, *The Michigan Chronicle* (Detroit, MI: Real Times Inc. 2007); Elihu Katz and Paul Felix Lazarsfeld, *Personal influence: the part played by people in the flow of mass communications* (New York: Free Press, 1955), 138.

[2] Even "close-out" politics describes a real and interesting form of politics – i.e., lame-ducks, term limited officials, retirements, and the like.

In the previous chapters we demonstrated the salutary effects of participating in deliberative retail politics. But given the scale of our sessions one might reasonably worry that retail politics will always be dwarfed by wholesale politics. We claim, however, that new communication technology allows for a kind of "discount" politics in the sense of greatly lowering the costs of participating in retail politics for constituents, and indeed for the elected officials themselves. In this chapter we show that the patterns reported in Chapters 3–6 "scale up" in a deliberative town hall with hundreds of participants, and in fact we have reason to believe that these effects could exist even for events in the thousands.[3]

Moreover, we have yet to consider the ways that one constituent's participation in a deliberative town hall might spark further discussion with others at different sites throughout the larger political system. We found that the constituents who participated in our larger session were so enthusiastic about the events that they talked about them with friends and family, and even tried to persuade others to support specific policies and candidates for office. In this way, the number of people indirectly affected by our event was larger than the number in the online deliberative town halls themselves. Thus, the events "scaled out" in addition to "scaling up," creating a multiplier effect that rippled through the deliberative system.

Taken together, our results suggest that there are reasons to be optimistic that directly representative institutions could affect hundreds and perhaps even thousands of people per deliberative town hall. And, moreover, with an hour or two of deliberative town halls per week for each member of Congress, there would be an accumulation of deliberative town halls that could reach millions of citizens each year, rather than thousands. Thus, unlike the stated goals of many mini-publics to stand-in for a deliberative citizenry, the aim of directly representative reforms is to lessen the tension between deliberative and participatory goals.[4]

A BIGGER DELIBERATIVE TOWN HALL

To study how our online platform scales up and out, we conducted an additional study that involved then-Senator Carl Levin (D-MI). In the

---

[3] This chapter draws on David M. Lazer et al., "Expanding the Conversation: Multiplier Effects From a Deliberative Field Experiment," *Political Communication* 32, no. 4 (2015): 552–73.

[4] This observation should reassure critics of mini-publics like Cristina Lafont, "Can Democracy be Deliberative & Participatory? The Democratic Case for Political Uses of Mini-Publics," *Daedalus* 146, no. 3 (2017): 85–105.

summer of 2008, we hosted an online deliberative town hall for Senator Levin and 175 of his constituents from Michigan, which was about seven times the average size of the sessions we conducted for members of the House of Representatives. Senator Levin chose the topic of terrorist detainee policy, which was both a prominent issue in the news at the time as well as an important topic for the Senator as chairman of the Committee on Armed Services. This study is therefore a double robustness check, addressing whether our prior results stand with a larger audience as well as across issues.

We used a survey firm to recruit 900 citizens from the state of Michigan to participate in the study.[5] Among these study participants, we invited a random subset of 462 people to participate in the online deliberative town hall with Senator Levin and the others were assigned to a control group. Of the 462 invited to the Levis session, 175 were able to participate. In order to isolate the impact of scale, we hewed as closely as possible to the structure of the immigration sessions with House members. Prior to the deliberative town hall, we provided participants with background reading materials, assembled from Congressional Research Service reports. We reproduce the reading material in the appendix to this chapter.[6] As in the previous study, we had two comparison groups of participants who did not participate in the deliberative town hall, one of which received the reading materials, and one of which did not. The one salient difference was that, unlike the House experiment, in this session we did not include a constituent-only chat, because the size of the group would have made it unwieldy.

SCALING UP?

The key *scaling up* question is whether we get similar results from this larger deliberative town hall as for the smaller ones presented in earlier chapters. Unlike face-to-face events, online deliberative town halls provide minimal cues as to the size of the audience. We have good reason

---

[5] Polimetrix, now YouGov, ran the recruitment for us. Because of cost constraints, we had to use a convenience sample, rather than one representative of the state as a whole. As a result, the participants were more politically active and aware than the smaller deliberative town halls we conducted with House members.

[6] "Treatment of US Detainees at Guantánamo Bay," *The American Journal of International Law* 99, no. 1 (2005): 261; and Jennifer K. Elseay, *Treatment of Battlefield Detainees in the War on Terrorism* (Congressional Research Service, updated 2007), Accessed May 29, 2018. https://fas.org/sgp/crs/terror/RL31367.pdf.

to expect that the results would indeed scale up. Consider the difference between a face-to-face event with twenty in attendance versus 20,000. The former could be in a living room, and the latter would require a stadium. The former setting would permit an interactive back and forth, and in the latter interactivity would seem absurd. Online, however, the experiences in the two cases could be designed to feel similar, except that the probability that a participant could pose a question that would be answered drops from above 50 percent to near zero in a very large event. And by this measure, 175 constituents participating in a forty-minute session is actually closer to 20,000 participants than to twenty – because in the time available, around a dozen questions could be addressed, for a ratio of about half for the deliberative town halls of size twenty, but only about 7 percent in the latter. Thus, the results we find for a deliberative town hall of 175 might plausibly generalize to online audiences much larger. To the constituent, however, the experience is similar if she asked an unanswered question in a deliberative town hall of any size.

In previous chapters, we documented how our deliberative town halls with members of the House of Representatives attracted a broad cross section of constituents, motivated the constituents to become better informed on the issue, led them to have a rational and substantive exchange, and left them feeling that the session was efficacious for them and beneficial for democracy. Do these same results scale up in the larger session we hosted with Sen. Levin? As we show next, the direct impacts of the larger session were consistent with the results we report from the smaller deliberative town halls.

Representativeness. We worked with a convenience sample for the larger session, and hence this study was not designed to test whether the event attracted a representative cross-section of Michigan's eligible voters. That said, we can examine the demographics of those who we invited to the demographics of those who participated to see whether there are strong differences between the sample that was invited and those who actually participated. We show in Table 7.1 that the participant pool indeed reflects the invitation pool in our sample, and this strongly suggests that, had we invited a representative group of participants, then the session participants would have been representative as well.

Knowledge gains. The surveys for this study contained five items measuring detainee policy knowledge, listed in Table 7.2. We administered these questions to all of our study participants (those invited to the deliberative town hall and those in the control groups), both before and after the deliberative town hall. We compare whether those who

TABLE 7.1. *Representativeness of participants in the study with Sen. Levin*

	Invited (%)	Attended (%)
Extreme/Quite interested in politics	78	79
Extremely likely to vote	84	86
Male	54	52
Democrat	37	34
Republican	29	29
White	86	87
Black	8	6
Hispanic	2	1
Asian	1	1
Native American	1	2
Other	3	3
Less than college degree	59	59

read the background materials and attended the session were more likely to answer these items correctly on the follow up survey compared to, respectively, those who only read the background materials and the true controls.

We find significantly more correct answers among those who participated in the session compared to those in the control groups, but on fewer items compared to the House study. Overall, compared to the true controls, the deliberative group participants on average were more likely to answer all five of the detainee items correctly, although only two at statistically significant levels. We note, however, that subjects in this study were much more politically knowledgeable to begin with, and were very likely to give a correct response on each of the detainee items on the pretest. There was simply less room for improvement compared to the immigration policy items. Because of this, the smaller treatment effects on the Levin experiment compared to the experiment involving House members are sensible and reasonably indicate knowledge gains among the deliberative town hall participants.

Persuasion, as captured by deliberative group participants changing preferences on the issue under discussion toward the representative's position, opinions regarding the representative, and increased probability of voting for the representative, were remarkably similar to the House sessions. In particular, we find that participants in the online deliberative

TABLE 7.2. *Detainee policy knowledge items*

1. Do you happen to know whether the United States has signed the Geneva Conventions (the international laws governing the treatment of people during wartime) and the United Nations Convention Against Torture?
   a) Only the Geneva Conventions
   b) Only the United Nations Convention Against Torture
   c) **Both (44 percent correct)**
2. The US military removed the Taliban from government in which country:
   a) Iraq
   b) Saudi Arabia
   c) **Afghanistan (71 percent correct)**
   d) Israel
3. Under US law and the United Nations Convention Against Torture, torture is legal:
   a) Only against citizens of countries who have not signed the treaty
   b) Only when both the President and a special court certify that there is a clear and present danger that requires it
   c) **Never, regardless of nationality, danger, or certification (79 percent correct)**
4. About how many captured people has the United States sent to the detention facility at Guantanamo Bay, Cuba?
   a) 50
   b) **500 (53 percent correct)**
   c) 2,000
   d) 5,000
5. The Bush Administration has argued that the President has the authority to hold some individuals captured during combat against the United States without trial and indefinitely. Do you happen to know whether or how the Supreme Court ruled on this issue?
   a) The Supreme Court has not ruled on the issue
   b) The Supreme Court has ruled in support of the Bush Administration's position
   c) **The Supreme Court has ruled against the Bush Administration's position (59 percent correct)**

Note: Boldface font indicates the correct answer and *pretreatment* percent correct.

town hall were about 10 percent more likely to agree with Levin's position on waterboarding, a topic that was frequently discussed in the session, compared to those who only received the background information.

In contrast, participants did not move toward Sen. Levin's position on the topic of closing Guantanamo prison, which was not discussed at the event, and thus served as our placebo test. As in the House study, we found substantial increases in trust, approval and the intent to vote in the upcoming November election, as well as the actual vote for Sen. Levin in the November election.

Satisfaction. We asked the participants their reactions to the session, with results that very closely reproduce those we found with the House study: 79 percent agreed the sessions were helpful and informative, and 30 percent indicated the sessions changed their position on a policy topic. About 95 percent stated that interactions such as those in our online deliberative town hall are valuable for democracy, and 98 percent stated that they would be interested in participating in a similar session on a different topic.

Overall, the encouraging findings we see in the House of Representatives study are mirrored in the larger group with Sen. Levin. The consistent findings also strongly suggest that the results are robust across different topics, different samples, a different interface, and different year. These results make us confident that we can make our deliberative town halls larger, and thus more likely to be felt in the larger political system. But we are interested in whether the deliberative town halls can also stimulate engagement with policy and politicians, even among citizens who do not get to participate directly.

SCALING OUT

How much do deliberative town halls reverberate through citizens' social networks?[7] Do participants talk to their spouses, friends, and coworkers about their experience? In order to answer these questions, we asked our participants whom they talk to about politics. Our initial survey asked everyone to identify the three people whom they talk to most about politics – that is, their political "discussants." A week after the session, we asked everyone to report recent conversations with their discussants. The question is whether participants in the deliberative town hall with Sen. Levin were more likely to talk with their discussants than people who had only read the background information.

For the 175 individuals who attended the session with Senator Levin, we received information on 521 discussants in their social networks (not every person named three contacts). We used this information to assess

---

[7] See James N. Druckman, Matthew S. Levendusky, and Audrey McLain, "No Need to Watch: How the Effects of Partisan Media Can Spread via Interpersonal Discussions," *American Journal of Political Science* 62, no. 1 (2017): 99–112.

the broader impact of the sessions. If participation in the deliberative town hall did not spur conversations with their three closest political discussants, then it seems quite unlikely that the event would have spurred substantial conversations with anyone. Conversely, if we do find "extra" discussion among close contacts, the amount provides a conservative estimate of the broader impact of the session, since we do not ask about conversations beyond those three ties, nor conversations amongst third parties (e.g., friends talking to *their* friends).

Before analyzing such deliberative ripples, we have to unpack the *what* and *who* of scaling out. First, *what* information might we expect participants to share with their discussants after the event? The deliberative town hall involved a *senator* talking about *policy*; in particular Sen. Levin's deliberative town hall focused on terrorist detainee policy. Second, to *whom* do we expect information to flow? The participants reported having different types of discussants – friends, relatives, coworkers – as well as different levels of agreement about politics.

Past research suggests that information flows through social networks,[8] but some research suggests that deliberation in particular draws out only shared knowledge across participants, rather than privately held experiences (the so-called "hidden profile effect"). So it is possible that participants in our deliberative town halls might be reluctant to discuss their own experiences from having participated in the session. In addition, complex information, like reasoning in the deliberative town halls, tends to disseminate far less than simple information.[9]

In order to get at what participants discussed in their social networks subsequent to the event, we asked about three types of politically related conversations: (1) talk about politics in general; (2) talk about detainee policy; (3) talk about Senator Levin.

Discussion patterns across these three topics differed substantially. Participating in the deliberative town hall increased discussion about detainee policy by about 81 percent and discussion about Sen. Levin by 50 percent. In contrast, there was no impact on discussions regarding

---

[8] The classic study is Mark S. Granovetter, "Strength of Weak Ties," *The American Journal of Sociology* 78, no. 6 (1973): 1360–80. See also Daniel P. Carpenter, Kevin M. Esterling, and David M. J. Lazer, "Friends, Brokers, and Transitivity: Who Informs Whom in Washington Politics?," *The Journal of Politics* 66, no. 1 (February 2004): 224–46.

[9] For the hidden profile effect, see Garold Stasser and William Titus, "Hidden Profiles: A Brief History," *Psychological Inquiry* 14, no. 3–4 (2003): 304–13; and that complex information disseminates far less efficiently than simple information because it requires multiple exposures, see Damon Centola and Michael Macy, "Complex Contagions and the Weakness of Long Ties," *The American Journal of Sociology* 113, no. 3 (2007): 702–34.

politics more generally. Participants shared their novel experiences from the session – that is, they discussed the two topics that the deliberative town hall provided direct information about (the issue and the Senator), but they did not discuss topics that went beyond their direct experience in the session (politics in general).

These results suggest that participation creates distinct and salient information – about the policy and the politician – which spreads through the network, unlike the "hidden profile" findings mentioned above. The results also show that participation powerfully influences conversations outside of the deliberative town hall.

Next, we address *from whom* the information flows: that is, who amongst participants were most likely to increase discussion about detainee policy and Sen. Levin? Some worry that deliberation may reproduce and even amplify existing political inequalities. As we have seen, such inequalities were either unaffected by or actually lessened by participation. However, even if deliberative inequality did not manifest within our deliberative town halls, it is plausible that they might arise outside of them, where signifiers of status are more salient.

We therefore test whether these positive ripple effects depend on an array of factors such as whether the participant tends to avoid conflict, or is interested in, knowledgeable about, and active in politics. In addition, we looked at whether gender, education, experiences with detention policy, and shared ideology with Sen. Levin affected discussion. With two minor exceptions, we find no evidence that these factors matter. Conflict avoidance and shared ideology have substantively small and statistically marginal effects. Otherwise the drive toward more discussion was very broad based.

There are several reasons to believe that the sessions' impact might also be uneven across *discussants*, in particular when the conversations partners disagree. There are tremendous benefits to having conversations across political divides. However, increasing polarization over the last generation leads citizens, by and large, to talk to people who already share their views.[10] If the extra discussion from deliberative town halls occurred primarily within echo chambers, however, their democratic value would be diminished.

---

[10] See Diana C. Mutz, "Cross-Cutting Social Networks: Testing Democratic Theory in Practice," *The American Political Science Review* 96, no. 01 (2002): 111–26; and Bill Bishop, *The Big Sort: Why the Clustering of Like-Minded America Is Tearing Us Apart* (New York: Houghton Mifflin Harcourt, 2009).

We therefore test whether the ripple effects we find are contingent on agreement with the discussant. We also examine whether the *kind* of relationship matters. Political information may diffuse differently when the discussant is a friend, spouse, relative, coworker, or neighbor. The frequency with which the pair discusses politics, and the discussants political knowledge may also be important. We find little evidence of differential effects across discussant types. Participants were slightly more likely to talk about Sen. Levin with their spouses. But more striking and encouraging, participants were slightly *more* likely to talk with people who had divergent opinions. These deliberative town halls, then, ramified quite broadly through the larger deliberative system.

CONCLUSION

We set ourselves three tasks in this chapter. First, we sought to determine whether the findings in Chapters 3–6 (showing that the deliberative town halls met our first four normative criteria) remained robust to variations in the topic, format, participant pool, technology, timing, and political context. They did.

Next, we sought to determine whether deliberative town halls could meet our fifth, and final, criterion for a viable reform proposal: that they could operate at a scale capable of affecting the larger deliberative system. The town halls scaled up quite well, showing little difference after increasing the size of the session by a factor of seven. Moreover, these effects would likely remain as the sessions scaled up even more, since we did not see any decline in the effects when the probability of being able to directly pose a question to the representative already dropped very low.

Further, the deliberative town halls scaled out, kindling a wider conversation regarding policy and elected officials. Participants talked about detainee policy and Sen. Levin at much higher rates. The added effect was considerable. While 175 people participated in the session, we estimate that they talked to another 254 about detention policy or Sen. Levin – a full 145 percent multiplier on the people who participated directly. And this is a conservative estimate since we only asked about three discussants, and we have no way of evaluating further ripples, for example, amongst the friends of friends.

Directly representative democracy need not be a marginal add-on to "real" politics. If each member of Congress were to spend just two hours a week fostering direct representation via deliberative town halls, in principle they could reach about a quarter of the voting eligible population of the United States directly every third Congress.[11] And that does not consider the multiplier effects of secondary and tertiary discussions or the potential for even larger deliberative town halls. Elected officials can and should conduct more of the nation's politics *with* the people.

APPENDIX: TERRORIST DETAINEE POLICY BACKGROUND MATERIALS

INTRODUCTION

Following the terrorist attacks of 9/11, Congress gave President Bush the power "to use all necessary and appropriate force" against anyone who "planned, authorized, committed, or aided the terrorist attacks" against "the United States." This began the war on terror. Soon thereafter, the United States invaded Afghanistan to overthrow their rulers, the Taliban, who had harbored and supported the terrorist group Al Qaeda. Then in 2003 the United States invaded Iraq.

THE WAR ON TERROR AND THE LAW

During the course of the war on terror the US government transferred about 520 captured people to the US Naval Station in Guantanamo Bay, Cuba, for detention and possible prosecution for war crimes. These detainees – designated "enemy combatants" – were not initially granted the ability to challenge their detention in front of a judge.

The Bush Administration has argued that the war on terror is a new kind of conflict, requiring a new set of rules for the detention and treatment of persons suspected of posing a terrorist threat. The US Constitution guarantees prisoners the right, known as *habeas corpus*, to challenge the legitimacy of their detention in a court of law. The Bush Administration

---

[11] In 2016, the voting eligible population in the United States was estimated to be 230,585,915. There are 535 members of Congress. If each did two sessions per week for six years that would work out to: $52 \times 2 \times 6 \times 535 =$ or 333,840 sessions $\times$ 175 people per session = 58,422,000 constituents reached. 58,422,000 / 230,585,915 = 25.3 percent of the voting eligible electorate reached. And that does not take into account even larger sessions or secondary effects.

has argued that the circumstances of the war on terror give the government the authority to detain certain individuals without trial.

In 2004, the Supreme Court ruled against this, arguing that "a state of war is not a blank check for the president" and that enemy combatants have the right to challenge their detention before a judge or other "neutral decision-maker."

The Department of Defense then established Combatant Status Review Tribunals to meet the requirements of the right to a trial. These tribunals determine whether Guantanamo detainees were "enemy combatants" who could be detained for the duration of the war on terror and prosecuted in military commissions for any war crimes committed.

The Combatant Status Review Tribunals are similar to the procedures the Army uses to determine Prisoner of War (POW) status during traditional wars. When a Tribunal determines that a detainee is no longer an enemy combatant, the detainee is usually transferred to their country of citizenship. Those deemed unlawful enemy combatants are given a chance to argue, in a separate proceeding before the Tribunal, that they should be released because they are no longer a threat.

The tribunals, so far, have not been bound by the rules of evidence used in civilian courts. They use classified information to try the detainees. The detainee is not given access to classified government evidence. Instead, each detainee is assigned a military officer, who would serve as their attorney, and only this officer could view the classified information.

In an effort to clarify legal issues surrounding the detention process, the Republican controlled Congress passed the Military Commissions Act (MCA) in 2006, which was subsequently signed into law by President Bush. This act tried to take away the jurisdiction of civilian courts to hear *habeas corpus* challenges by Guantanamo detainees based on their treatment or living conditions.

After the Democrats regained majorities in both the House and Senate in 2006, the Senate Judiciary Committee sent The Habeas Corpus Restoration Act of 2007 to the full Senate in June of 2007. This legislation would restore the *habeas corpus* rights of detainees.

However, the Supreme Court ruled in *Boumediene* v. *Bush* that the 2006 MCA law setting up the tribunals was unconstitutional. Further, the Court ruled that the detainees have habeas corpus rights under the Constitution, and that the system the administration had put in place to classify them as enemy combatants and review those decisions was inadequate.

TREATMENT OF DETAINEES

The United States is party to both the Geneva Conventions and the United Nations Convention against Torture. These international laws govern the treatment of civilians and combatants during wartime. The treaties give captured individuals who are affiliated with foreign armed forces special status known as Prisoners of War (POW). The United Nations Convention against Torture prohibits torture under all circumstances and for any reason, and holds individuals responsible for violations of these prohibitions, regardless of orders from governments, courts, or superiors.

The US Detainee Treatment Act of 2005 requires uniform standards for interrogation and expressly bans cruel, inhuman, or degrading treatment of detainees in the custody of any US agency. The interpretation of these prohibitions is largely linked to practices that would be prohibited under the Fifth, Eighth, and Fourteenth Amendments to the US Constitution.

While US courts and administrative bodies have found that severe beatings, sexual assault, rape, and (in certain circumstances) death threats may constitute "torture," courts have not decided whether harsh, yet sophisticated, interrogation techniques of lesser severity (e.g., "waterboarding") constitute "torture" under either international treaties or US law.

Meanwhile the United States' treatment of detainees who remain in custody continues to be a source of contention with human rights groups and other nations. Photographs depicting the apparent abuse of Iraqi detainees at the hands of US military personnel at Abu Ghraib prison in Iraq have resulted in numerous investigations, congressional hearings, and prosecutions, raising questions regarding the applicable law. Some critics contend that US policy effectively continues to permit harsh treatment that falls below international standards.

Conclusion

Republican Redux

> At the close of the constitutional convention a lady asked Benjamin Franklin: "Well, Doctor, what have we got — a Republic or a Monarchy?" Franklin replied: "A Republic — if you can keep it."
>
> —James McHenry

Today we may be apt to read this anecdote as a gently cynical joke. After all, Americans have managed to keep their republic for almost two and a half centuries now. But at the time, Franklin was surely quite serious, if witty, in expressing his concern. History to that point suggested that republics were unstable, especially at scale, and that democracies were prone to degenerating into tyranny. For many citizens those dormant concerns have begun to resurface. Invoking Franklin's quip expresses urgent, not gentle, cynicism, and, if it is a joke, it is gallows humor. Post-truth politics leads to pre-authoritarian governance.[1] Even many of those for whom it may seem overheated to talk of losing our republic worry with Pitkin that "The arrangements we call 'representative democracy' have become a substitute for popular self-government, not its enactment."[2] The banality of tyranny, perhaps.

On either the urgent or banal reading, representative democracy is nevertheless in trouble. Confidence and trust in our democratic institutions is at an all-time low. Average citizens do not feel motivated and empowered to participate in their own self-governance; cynicism and apathy flow from a rigged system and scorched-earth partisan warfare.

---

[1] Timothy Snyder, *On Tyranny: Twenty Lessons from the Twentieth Century* (New York: Tim Duggan Books, 2017).
[2] Pitkin, "Representation and Democracy: Uneasy Alliance."

In response, proposals abound for making representative democracy either less representative or less democratic. Going alternatives in the institutional status quo just cycle around: technocracy creates democratic deficits; populist nationalism threatens rights; direct democracy ends up empowering vested interests at least as much as the status quo; and doubling down on interest-group pluralism encourages citizens to act as consumers, with parties turning voting and elections into little more than tribal antagonism.

While our focus has been on the United States, many democracies around the world exhibit the same array of symptoms. The Internet, identified by early techno-optimists as a boon for democracy, actually seems to be accelerating many of these dangerous trends. Social media and social algorithms enable people to sink into their respective bubbles, connecting only with the like-minded, seeing only (sometimes fake) news that resonates with predispositions.

With *directly representative democracy* we propose instead to strengthen both the representative and democratic elements simultaneously – to *expand* representative democracy's potential in good times and in bad. Rather than concede to a cycle of zero sum lurches between reform movements that do not cut to the root of the problem, we propose building more direct and deliberative connections between citizens and government officials that would be a boon in any context. But such connections are especially urgent as an alternative to our broken system of interest-group rent seeking and partisan intransigence. Building them will go some way toward reconnecting citizens to their government *as citizens*, rather than merely as consumers or tribal combatants.

Directly representative democracy is *direct* in that it bypasses and supplements the highly mediated pathways of interest groups, parties, and mass media that constitute status quo politics. It is *representative* in that it strengthens established representative institutions rather than attempting to work around them. And it is *democratic* in that citizens play a robust role through all phases of the political process, rather than simply showing up every four years to render an up or down judgment.

Nor is our proposal merely notional. Instead, it is based on a series of groundbreaking experiments which evaluated an alternative conception of democracy in a realistic, yet scientifically rigorous, way. Members of Congress agreed to be randomly assigned to samples of their constituents, participating in online town-hall meetings about some of the most important and controversial issues of the day. The results reveal a model of how our democracy could work, where politicians consult with and inform citizens in substantive discussions, and where otherwise marginalized citizens participate and feel empowered. Our evidence suggests that with modest reforms and resources, we can reinvest substantially in the deliberative infrastructure of our politics.

Some may worry that we have an overly optimistic vision of human potential. Many argue that both human nature and the practicalities of mass democracy restrict the role that average citizens can play in self-government to periodic opportunities to remove elites from power. Such arguments extend beyond the empirical and policy domains. In recent years democratic theory has been preoccupied with debates regarding so called "ideal" versus "non-ideal" or "realist" political theory. We believe that such arguments have been somewhat miscast. In most cases the conflict is not between views anchoring the idealistic and realistic poles. After all, the noted philosopher John Rawls, often treated as the arch-ideal-theorist, extensively engaged the social scientific literature of his day, and on that basis argued for his "realistic" utopia. And conversely, most leading realists hardly reincarnate Machiavelli. Rather the debate hinges on: (1) how practical constraints should guide our norms and institutions, and (2) how malleable putative facts about politics and human nature really are. Herein lies one of our contributions to democratic theory.

Given the evidence presented above, our proposals do not require starry-eyed idealism to warrant their promise. Thus, defeatism about the putatively tribal nature of politics is unwarranted. Parties and interest groups do not exhaust the domain of the political in modern democracy. Instead, we agree with James Madison, who provided both a more balanced vision of citizens' capacities, as well as practical reasons to extend a modicum of faith in the potential of democratic governance:

As there is a degree of depravity in mankind which requires a certain degree of circumspection and distrust, so there are other qualities in human nature which justify a certain portion of esteem and confidence. Republican government presupposes the existence of these qualities in a higher degree than any other form. Were the pictures which have been drawn by the political jealousy of some among us faithful likenesses of the human character, the inference would be, that there is not sufficient virtue among men for self-government. (Madison, Federalist No.55).

For Madison, institutional innovation was the key to promoting the parts of human nature that justify "esteem and confidence."

BUT CAN IT REALLY WORK?

We have argued for reviving republicanism by augmenting current political practices with directly representative institutions. Many prominent critics of deliberation have argued, however, that well-intended reforms to enhance deliberation in contemporary democracy are misguided and potentially even harmful. Recall that John Hibbing, Elizabeth Theiss-Morse, Richard Posner, and many others claim that Americans are unwilling to deliberate, and that asking them to do so is paternalistic and counterproductive. They note that almost half of eligible citizens fail even to vote. It would seem unreasonable to expect that citizens would want to make the greater effort (or have the capacity) to engage in much more demanding democratic practices such as deliberative town halls. Still other critics argue that deliberative institutions can magnify inequalities already present in society.

As we have seen, these critics implicitly subscribe to an overly narrow theory of democracy that mistakenly takes the status quo as given. We have demonstrated, to the contrary, that legislators and citizens alike have a preference for a more directly representative democracy and that the alternative we describe can make democracy more constructive – that both citizens and legislators find this alternative highly rewarding.

We have shown that online technology enables directly representative encounters that draw a much better cross section of constituents than usual, which, in turn, drives very different behaviors on the part of both constituents and representatives. Our deliberative town halls attracted a diverse group of citizens, who became informed on the issue, and who engaged reasonably, respectfully, and rationally. In addition, the deliberative town halls enhanced trust among participants of all walks of life, and scaled up to a meaningful size.

In Chapter 3 we asked who wants to participate in directly representative institutions. Some argue that most Americans want nothing to do with a more directly representative democracy and that such reticence is reasonable. If so, cajoling citizens into more consultative participation would be paternalistic and even counterproductive. But our central premise – that much nonparticipation is rooted in disaffection with status quo politics – was borne out. So current patterns of engagement do not reflect how citizens would participate given more attractive opportunities. The profile of those willing to participate in direct representation is markedly different from those who participate in standard partisan politics and interest-group pluralism. This profile suggests that average citizens do not seem to regard such opportunities as filigree on "real" politics nor as an indulgence meant only for political activists and intellectuals. Quite the opposite: they have a widespread, if latent, desire for more directly representative participation.

Even if many regular citizens are interested in directly democratic representation, one may still question whether institutional innovation can overcome widespread voter ignorance, and so whether citizens have the capacity to engage in deliberative exchanges effectively. In Chapter 4 we addressed such concerns. Directly representative democrats claim that so called "rational ignorance" about politics is less a matter of free-riding than a perception that staying informed about politics is a fool's errand. If "real" politics is only a matter of interest-group pluralism and partisan warfare, then there is little reason for average citizens to expend the effort on a rigged game. Citizens need a more persuasive set of motives and opportunities to stay informed. We claim that consultation provides both the motive and the opportunity. We assessed this claim, finding that constituents demonstrate a strong capacity to become informed in response to these opportunities. Participants increased their attention to policy outside the context of the experiment because they perceived that elected officials actually cared about what they thought. Moreover, their capacity for motivated learning seems to be widespread. It is unrelated to standard demographics and prior political knowledge.

Even if citizens learn factual information via participation, are they willing to engage each other and their representatives in a constructive, reason-giving conversation? We concede that, to date, research casts serious doubt on claims that standard town hall meetings serve rational public deliberation. In Chapter 5 we analyzed persuasion on substantive issues in our own deliberative town halls, focusing on a heated and important issue of the day: immigration policy. We contrast the constructive discourse in our sessions with traditional town hall meetings, held by many of the same representatives, at the same time, on the same issue, and this contrast helps reinforce just how different our directly representative institutions are from contemporary practices. We showed that representatives offer reasonable explanations for their policy positions; constituents are generally open to being persuaded by these carefully constructed arguments; and the representatives themselves report that the deliberative town halls are valuable opportunities to consult with their constituents.

In Chapter 6 we addressed whether the constituents and the members of Congress thought the deliberative town halls were constructive enough to be worth doing more often. Obviously both would have to judge them positively to take the idea to scale. The evidence on the constituent side is very clear, with overwhelming majorities judging the events to be a success, and saying that they would like to do more of them. Moreover, using this new online "home style," we show that representatives were able to persuade constituents to more favorable views of the representatives themselves, as well as change their political behavior. Importantly, we found that neither participation nor satisfaction were significantly related to the participants' gender, race, age or education level. Thus, directly democratic reforms have the promise to increase the "intimate sympathy" between average citizens and their representatives that the Founders thought so necessary for free government to flourish.

For their part, representatives may have been hesitant to criticize any form of interaction with their constituents. That said, nearly all of the evidence suggests that the representatives enjoyed the sessions and found them to be a good way to interact with their constituents. In addition, our results show that the constituents who participated were more likely to vote for the representative in the future, which is a fundamental goal of nearly all elected officials. Thus, directly representative democracy creates a virtuous circle in which representatives do well for themselves by engaging with their constituents in a genuine, unscripted two-way conversation. But would such events work on a larger scale, and so be a worthwhile investment in time and resources for representatives and the larger polity?

Even fellow reformers might doubt that our results scale up to a level that could actually affect mass politics perceptibly. We addressed such worries in Chapter 7 by running a larger session, and linking information on the people's social networks with their participation in the experiments. Those who attended the deliberative session dramatically increased their political discussion among friends, relatives, and coworkers on topics relating to the event. Importantly, we also found that participants from all backgrounds and walks of life engaged in these broader discussions. This finding provides reassurance that the positive spillovers from the sessions into everyday life are not limited to certain portions of the citizenry. Thus, even relatively small-scale encounters have broader, egalitarian effects among the mass public.

A (REMAINING) QUESTION CONCERNING TECHNOLOGY

We designed these online deliberative town halls with particular normative objectives in mind, but there is nothing in our plan that coerces members of Congress to adhere to our recommendations or to foster more widespread deliberation. Indeed, we observe that nowadays representatives often use social media and other online communication channels in ways that selectively mobilize their base and sometimes even provide self-serving misinformation to constituents. We do not doubt that online deliberative town halls might be used to bamboozle and confuse, to control the conversation, to prevent or stifle criticism and dissent.

Indeed, there is reason to be concerned. In 2009, when we released a preliminary report on these findings, some on the political right objected that those on the left would use these events to evade citizens protesting their support for the Affordable Care Act. Ironically, as we complete this book, there are widespread accusations from the left that those on the right are using telephone town halls – a sibling of online town halls – as a means to avoid confrontation with their constituents protesting their support for *repeal* of the Affordable Care Act.

More generally, expectations surrounding technology and democracy have ranged from utopian in the 1990s – focusing on the possibilities of the Internet to vastly broaden the participation of citizens, to inform, and to enlighten – to dystopian in 2018, where the Internet is seen as dominated by trolls, fake news, and filter bubbles. Domestically, the Internet is tightly regulated in China, and it facilitated Russian electoral interference abroad.

We want to push back against, but not lightly dismiss, the current dystopian vision. Much as iron can be pounded into swords or into ploughshares, the Internet can both serve and thwart democratic aims. It has enabled trolls, but it has also empowered collaboration, citizen science, Wikipedia, and other valuable innovations. Directly representative democracy implies a set of design standards for how to use the Internet to promote specific democratic goods – to enable substantive conversation between citizens and their representatives.

Specifically, those seeking successful consultation should:

- *Recruit a broad audience and adopt ground rules and technology that encourage equal participation.* This recommendation follows on our first standard to ensure that a diverse, inclusive cross-section of the community engages in the session. In our case, we were successful in recruiting a representative cross section of constituents, and procedurally we posted each question in the order they arrived, only filtering for redundancy and to prioritize those who had not yet spoken up.

- *Focus on a single or small number of timely and relevant issues, and provide balanced background information on the issue(s) in advance.* We show that when citizens have the motive and opportunity to learn about policy they do, and so can engage in the discussion in a more confident and informed manner.
- *Recruit a neutral moderator who uses clear ground rules.* Having a trusted moderator who is not connected to the representative's office will improve the chances that the participants will view the event as a space for free expressions of their ideas, rather than as an infomercial. On a larger scale, we could even imagine a commission on deliberative town halls (like the one on debates) which could provide moderators, choose topics, and curate background materials.
- *Focus on unscripted, real-time interaction*: When representatives engage in unscripted, real-time conversations with their constituents, they demonstrate respect for their constituents' views, that in turn enhances the representatives' presentation of self, fostering warranted trust in the representative relationship. Hearing the representatives' voice (and perhaps seeing streaming video) reassures constituents that they are connecting directly with the representative, rather than to a staff person.

A town hall that incorporates all of these design features is likely to meet the standards that we set out in Chapter 1, and to foster directly representative democracy in practice. Over time, as citizens gain experience with directly representative practices, we believe that they will embrace these standards and come to expect them.

PROSPECTS GOING FORWARD

Our evidence suggests that both elected officials and their constituents can buy into these design standards. We are not merely proposing that citizens and politicians eat their spinach, cajoling representatives and citizens to do the right thing against their interests. The citizens who participated enjoyed the events, found them to be highly valuable, and indicated an interest in participating again; the representatives saw their approval ratings and vote share improve substantially. The forum evoked the better angels of democracy: we did not observe a single instance of trolling amongst the citizens, nor any significant misinformation from the representatives. Thus, representatives can "do well by doing right."

And citizens win all around as well. They experience increased respect, and generate broader democratic goods as a result. Directly representative practices are thus realistic, and create gains for democracy on every dimension.[3]

The representatives consistently expressed such sentiments in their closing remarks, praising the sessions as an opportunity to enhance and strengthen the representative relationship. For example, Congressman Radanovich (R, CA-19) said:

Excellent questions. I've got to tell you, I really enjoy this new technology that enables us to talk, enables me to talk to my constituents back home, and I hope that this is something that we can expand upon and as this technology grows, maybe we can do face to face. But thank you to everybody who participated. And I hope, hope it was enlightening.

From Congressman Kingston (R, GA-1):

I think Connecting to Congress [the original name of the study] is a good project. In today's busy society, this is probably the most convenient way for everybody to attend a town meeting.

From Congressman Blumenauer (D, OR-3):

Well, I appreciate the opportunity to have this online discussion ... We're happy to explore with you ways that we can have more opportunities to be able to exchange views and share information and that hopefully out of this also there will be information that will help me better understand some of the concerns and questions that people have and together we can make this system work a little bit better.

The representatives appreciated the benefits of conducting the town halls according to our design. Newer technologies will only enhance those benefits.

One might reasonably worry, however, that elected officials could engineer seemingly deliberative events that provide them electoral benefits, without also generating the democratic benefits: for example, a Potemkin town hall, where questions (and even participants) were prescreened, and the representative presented prepared answers. There is reason to believe that such staging happens, but also that it is obvious to constituents when it does. In our study the participants repeatedly emphasized

---

[3] Boeckmann and Tyler, "Trust, respect, and the psychology of political engagement."

their appreciation for having an unmediated, unscripted exchange. Constituents were wary of "informercials," but emphatically judged our sessions as different, giving the representatives enormous credit for eschewing the staging and manipulation. Paradoxically, then, the urge to control the communication environment can backfire. Potemkin town halls, therefore, would likely reduce the political benefits to participating representatives.

IS NOW THE TIME?

"While confined here in the Birmingham city jail, I came across your recent statement calling my present activities 'unwise and untimely.'" Thus, Martin Luther King Jr. launched his great epistle on political protest, rejoining those moderate white ministers who rebuked him for abandoning deliberation and negotiation in favor of disruption. Extraordinary injustice justifies extraordinary politics, Dr. King explained. Many people today fervently believe that we live in similarly extraordinary times, and call again for extraordinary politics. Indeed, such calls for extraordinary politics hail from all over the political landscape.

Black Lives Matter highlights the ways in which urgent racial injustices that motivated the civil rights movement remain urgent. The Tea Party formed out of fears that the federal government's growing reach stifles economic dynamism and threatens the prerequisites of a free society. Indivisible and the Occupy movement coalesced from corresponding fears that corporate plutocracy was eroding democratic norms of equality and the rule of law. The Never Trump movement suborned unfaithful delegates, rebelling against its own party's standard bearer. And Trump himself drew support from those who wanted to radically disrupt establishment politics generally. All of these groups claim the kind of urgency, enormity, and moral clarity that justify disruption over deliberation.

Readers of very different political stripes might therefore worry that the reforms proposed in this book – which focus on improving the deliberative quality of ordinary politics – are altogether "untimely." Now is not the moment, you might say, to emphasize dialogue and deliberation. At best, we are naive and complacent, rearranging deck chairs on a sinking ship of state. At worst, we abet a fundamentally broken system.

Yet, despite appearances, Dr. King affirmed the priority of deliberative politics. While languishing unjustly in a jail cell for engaging in disruptive action, he responds with a remarkable enactment of higher-order deliberative politics, one that justifies and delimits the conditions of extraordinary politics: "Since I feel that you are men of genuine good will and that your criticisms are sincerely set forth, I want to try to answer your statement in what I hope will be patient and reasonable terms." The subtlety and sublimity of Dr. King's reply emerge from the way that he fused the rational persuasion of the text with the moral suasion of its context. The letter itself is a brilliant contribution to deliberative politics, penned under wildly inauspicious circumstances.

We should not be surprised to find deliberative politics at the heart of the civil rights movement. From the perch of history, we tend to focus on the acts of civil disobedience themselves, rather than on how the protesters justified and prepared for them. We are tempted to see the justification as obvious, and the preparation as a formality. Yet that is precisely because the leaders of the movement were explicit and exacting about both: "In any nonviolent campaign there are four basic steps: collection of the facts to determine whether injustices exist; negotiation; self purification; and direct action." Knowing that police dogs, fire hoses, night sticks, and jail cells would follow on their actions rendered such careful progression anything but obvious and perfunctory.

Dr. King believed that any political movement that could withstand the scrutiny of history would first need to re-engage in deliberation informed by the facts collected, before considering disruption. But more importantly, any successful movement must aim to *restore* deliberative politics on terms that are more just and inclusive: "You may well ask: 'Why direct action? Why sit ins, marches and so forth? Isn't negotiation a better path?' You are quite right in calling for negotiation. Indeed, this is the very purpose of direct action… Too long has our beloved Southland been bogged down in a tragic effort to live in monologue rather than dialogue." Done well, disruption and deliberation can work together to deepen democracy. After enduring the dogs and night-sticks, John Lewis stood for a seat in Congress.

We leave it for each reader to judge which of today's rallying cries meet Dr. King's criteria. We submit that the directly democratic reforms of ordinary politics that we propose remain vital whatever you decide. Even if our proposals were to succeed beyond our highest ambitions, they would of course still pale next to the civil rights movement's epochal achievements. And we evince none of its leaders' moral courage in proposing them. Nevertheless, they share in the same vision of building a democratic community rooted in equality, freedom, justice, and mutual understanding. To those who worry that directly democratic reforms are untimely, then, our reply echoes Dr. King's concern that in politics, "'Wait' has almost always meant 'Never.'" Our republic can scarcely afford further delay.

Afterword

A Memo to Members of Congress

To: Representative Jane Doe
From: John Smith, Communications Director
Date: 1/1/2019
Re: Conducting new online deliberative town halls

Executive summary: This memo assesses the potential of conducting a specific kind of online deliberative town hall for connecting with constituents, as proposed in the book *Politics* with *the People: Building a Directly Representative Democracy*. The authors show that well-implemented online deliberative town halls can be very effective at building trust, approval, and votes, and can be scaled to have an expansive impact. This "directly representative" approach could revolutionize how you connect with your constituents. However, it comes with some unknowns. My recommendation is to do a handful of such events to assess how effective they are for you.

Summary of proposal: The essential idea is to consult with constituents as individual citizens, rather than merely as members of interest groups or political parties. You would meet with a broad range of constituents in an online deliberative town hall, moderated by a neutral party. We would employ simple group meeting technology often used by companies to facilitate team collaboration. Your constituents would be personally invited via an email from the office (or the moderator), providing a unique link to a meeting. The moderator would manage the flow of questions with a light hand.

Pros: This is a way of reaching out to constituents you rarely reach. Most constituents do not even know your name, and the few constituents that make it to your regular town halls do not reflect your broader district. They are more likely to be at the extremes ideologically and do not represent the diversity of your district. The same holds true of email and call-in campaigns to the office. While it is very important to listen to those voices, it is crucial to reach out to a broader swath of the district as well. *These deliberative town halls will provide you with input from a much better cross section of your constituents, especially those who do not contact you directly.* Unlike most of those who reach out to the office unprompted, participants in these deliberative town halls are persuadable. The research shows that these deliberative town halls will substantially increase your popularity amongst participants, increase their trust in you, and increase their likelihood of voting for you. *The average level of trust in Members jumped twelve points for participants, and the likelihood of voting for the Member conducting the deliberative town hall went up ten points* (months later). Remarkably, this is also true for constituents of the opposing party. These results are all the more impressive given recent findings that advertising and campaign contact are largely ineffective at persuading voters. The main exception to this "zero persuasion" is personal contact by candidates, like that proposed here.

Online deliberative town halls are a very cost-effective way to personally reach many constituents. The technology is virtually free. Your most valuable asset is your time, and online deliberative town halls take much less than other forms of personal contact with constituents, because there is no travel involved. You could conduct these deliberative town halls wherever you are, as long as there is reliable Internet. In principle, *you could directly connect with tens of thousands of voters per year,* at a cost of an hour or two of your time each week, where those town halls might spur conversations with tens of thousands more. Over a few terms, it is possible to connect with most of your constituents.

Cons: There are a number of uncertainties about the online deliberative town halls. First, it is uncertain how effective you will be at this format. This concern is mitigated by the fact that *every* Member who participated experienced improvement in their approval, trust, and voting numbers. Further, if you conduct a few of these deliberative town halls and you are uncomfortable in the format, we can cease conducting them. Second, because of the nature of the events, you have to assume that everything you say will be captured and recorded, and potentially used against you in a campaign. However, the potential of being recorded must now be assumed about everything you do in public (or even in private meetings).

Ingredients for a successful online deliberative town hall: The book's authors suggest several key ingredients for conducting a successful deliberative town hall. The most critical ingredient is your personal involvement – it is hearing your voice, and your direct responses to constituent questions that make these events compelling. Light-handed moderation – ideally from a neutral third party – increases the authenticity of the experience for constituents. Providing some short, nonpartisan factual materials to participants will improve the quality of the discussion, and highlight that it is not a campaign or partisan event. Recruiting a diverse set of constituents to participate in the deliberative town hall will provide you with a better signal of where your constituents, as a whole, stand. Finally, it is crucial to allow the moderator to select challenging questions for you to answer, and you should answer them directly. The findings from the study strongly suggest that constituents value unscripted and honest exchanges, and constituents from both political parties will respect you for doing so. If you do not know enough on a topic to provide an answer, say so. Staff will follow up with more information so you can respond most effectively.

Recommendation: There is considerable upside to conducting directly representative outreach like these online deliberative town halls. Conducting such events regularly could revolutionize your communication with constituents, radically increasing the number that feel personally connected to you. The potential downsides appear considerably smaller. We could easily assess them with some pilot events, and the cost of conducting pilots will be minimal. My strong recommendation is to set up some pilot events as soon as the schedule allows.

Appendix on Statistical Methods for Causal Inference

Above, we empirically evaluated the merits of our online deliberative town hall platform as a means to engage members of Congress and their constituents in a meaningful dialogue on important policy matters. Specifically, we test whether our platform measures up to the five standards that we set out in Chapter 1: first whether the online platform attracts a diverse cross section of the representative's constituency; and then whether participating in the deliberative town hall enhances constituents' policy knowledge, induces persuasive, rational discourse, and engenders trust and legitimacy; and finally whether the platform scales up to engage enough constituents to have an impact on democratic practice. To the extent our platform performs well by these standards, we can recommend it as a best practice for elected officials to use as part of everyday democratic representation.

Each of the five standards, however, poses a different kind of question for us to answer. The first standard asks whether, as a descriptive matter, the types of people who show up to an online deliberative town hall, when invited, are representative of the community from which they come. To answer the question posed by this standard, we only need to observe the correlation between the attributes of the constituents and their propensity to participate. In a statistical sense, observing these correlations is straightforward and the results are described in Chapter 3.

The fifth standard also presents a descriptive question: do the findings from the first study replicate when we increase the number of constituents. We describe this replication study in Chapter 7.

The middle three standards, however, imply a very different kind of question. That is, whether participation *caused* participants' knowledge gains, attitude changes, and political behavior. We test these claims in Chapters 4 through 6. In a statistical sense, testing for causal effects is significantly more challenging than evaluating an association or describing a replication. To demonstrate a causal effect, we need to compare what happened to the participants when exposed to the platform, to what *would* have happened to the same participants had they not been exposed to the platform (Rubin 1974, Holland 1986): a counterfactual world that we can never observe directly.[1]

In order to evaluate the causal impact of our platform on the participants, we used an experimental design that exposed some participants to the platform, and reserved other participants to two different control groups who were not exposed to the platform. Provided participants in the control groups are similar to those in the treatment group, other than exposure to the treatment, then their outcomes are comparable across the treatment and control groups, and so we can use the outcomes in each group to "fill in" the missing data that we need to evaluate the counterfactual and to assess the causal impact of our platform. In the general case we do not know which (if any) participants in the treatment group are identical to which participants in the control group, and so we cannot identify the treatment effect for each individual. Instead, we can use methods that ensure that on average the collections of participants are

---

[1] Donald Rubin, "Estimating causal effects of treatments in randomized and nonrandomized studies," *Journal of Educational Psychology* 66, no. 5 (1974) 688–701; Paul Holland, "Statistics and Causal Inference," *Journal of the American Statistical Association* 81, no. 396 (1986) 945–60. The statistician Donald Rubin developed the "potential outcomes" framework as a way to formalize this conception of causality as the effect that an intervention has on an individual's outcome in comparison to the outcome that same individual would have had if not exposed to the intervention. In the potential outcomes framework, each participant in an experiment potentially could be assigned to either the treatment condition or to the control condition, so conceptually has a potential outcome in each of the two states. The causal effect of the intervention for that individual is the contrast between her potential outcome in the two states. The key problem, which Holland (1986) labels the "fundamental problem of causal inference," is that the same individual can never be in the two conditions at the same time and so both potential outcomes cannot be observed in a given experiment. Instead, since the participant can enroll in only one of the two conditions, she will reveal her potential outcome in that condition but not the other, so in any evaluation of a causal effect, half of the data needed for the analysis must be missing. Solutions to the problem of causal inference make use of a research design that assigns similar people to both conditions so that the potential outcomes revealed by each group are comparable.

similar across treatment and control groups, and so we can identify the differences on average across the two groups.

In our research design, we made use of the classical experimental method based on random assignment of participants to treatment and control groups. In the ideal research setting, using random assignment assures that the participants in the treatment and control groups are systematically the same, except for exposure to the treatment, and so any differences in outcomes between the treatment and control groups can only be due to the treatment rather than to differences in the types of people in the two groups. This is the same design that clinical studies use to evaluate the effectiveness of a new drug, in which some participants are assigned to the "treatment" group and take the new drug, and others to a "control" group that takes a placebo (sugar pill) or takes the non-experimental drug that is currently in clinical use.

To see how random assignment works for our study, consider Figure 2.2, which we have reproduced in Figure A.1 (with a few modifications that we will discuss shortly). Recall that we have three comparison groups: a "treatment" group that reads the background material and participates in the deliberative town hall (the deliberative group or DG); a "control" group that only reads the background materials but does not participate in the deliberative town hall (the information-only group or IO); and another "control" group that neither reads the background materials nor participates in the deliberative town hall (the true control group or TC).

Imagine that for each participant we rolled a fair six-sided die. If the roll yielded a one or a two we would assign the participant to DG, a three or four to IO, or a five or six to TC. Under this procedure, there would

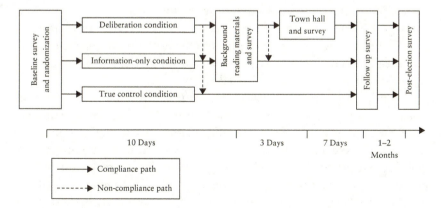

FIGURE A.1. *The experimental design for the House of Representatives study*

be no systematic differences between the participants assigned to each group. In practice, we used a computer to do the random assignment, but the computer program had the identical properties of a die roll for this assignment method.

Imagine instead if we did not use random assignment to create our comparison groups, and instead allowed the participants to choose which of the three treatment conditions they preferred to enroll into. In that case, one would suspect that the participants who chose the DG condition might be different in some ways from those who opted for the control groups, perhaps being the most politically active, or trusting, or knowledgeable. And if that were true, a comparison between the treatment and control groups regarding the relative knowledge or trust or a range of other outcomes would show a difference between the groups, but that difference would be due at least in part, if not entirely, to the differences between the kinds of people who select into each condition rather than the causal effect of the platform itself.

Under ideal experimental conditions, randomization can create comparison groups that are systematically similar to each other, but this ideal is difficult to attain in many ways. First, it is possible that the randomization itself affects the participants in some way that can make the groups not comparable, a violation of the so-called "exclusion restriction." For example, if participants know they had the opportunity to speak with their member of Congress in the DG condition, but got assigned instead to one of the control conditions where they are denied the opportunity, it is possible they could become discouraged about engaging in politics, or reduce their trust in government or the representative, simply because of their randomized assignment. Conversely, those assigned to speak with their representative might feel they won the lottery and so might be especially positive about participating in politics and toward their representative. In the presence of these responses to the randomization, it is possible that the outcomes of the two comparison groups would be different, even if the DG intervention had no actual effect.

Second, it is possible that the participants can communicate with each other across the treatment and control groups, and so create treatment spillovers. For example, if the DG induced greater knowledge among DG participants, and then DG participants were able to communicate that new knowledge to the participants in one of the control groups, both groups would appear relatively knowledgeable. This increase would be due to the DG intervention, but we would have little evidence to show the DG effect since there would be little contrast to the control group.

These two complications to our experimental design, violations of either the exclusion restriction or spillovers or both, can occur in any experimental study and, as is true in most experimental research, we are not able to test directly for their presence or absence in our study. As a result, we have to assume that these complications did not arise in our study. We feel these assumptions are easy for us to justify in our case. Regarding the exclusion restriction, while it is true that participants could be disappointed or have a similar reaction from not being selected to participate in the DG group, and vice versa for those selected to the DG group, we do not believe that this assignment would be momentous enough either way to significantly affect the responses of the participants. And regarding spillover, the participants were extremely unlikely to be in communication across the experimental conditions since they were anonymous, unlikely to know each other, and distributed across a large congressional district.

It is also possible for participants to fail to comply with the activities required for their randomized experimental group assignment. This complication is illustrated in Figure A.1 with the dotted lines, which we label the "non-compliance" paths. If participants do comply with their assignments, then they follow the solid lines through the experimental protocol, and under randomization and the two assumptions we mention above, the participants who comply with the protocol are systematically comparable to each other. Oftentimes in doing experimental research in the field, however, participants have the autonomy to choose not to comply with the protocol. As researchers we do not have either ethical or practical means to prevent them from doing so. In our study, it is possible for participants in the DG and IO conditions to choose not to read the background materials and so reassign themselves to the TC condition at that stage (the first downward dotted arrow non-compliance path in Figure A.1). In addition, participants assigned to the DG condition could read the background materials but fail to attend their assigned deliberative town hall, and so reassign themselves to the IO condition (the second downward dotted arrow path).

In addition, participants choose whether or not to respond to the follow up survey. The follow up survey contained a battery of questions measuring participants' knowledge of immigration policy, their preferences regarding various immigration policies, their levels of approval and trust, their self-efficacy, and many of the other outcomes that help us measure whether the online platform meets the standards for directly representative best practices. Even if all participants complied with their experimental protocol, if some participants in one of the experimental groups chose not to respond to the survey, the remaining participants in that group would no longer be comparable to those in the other conditions.

Statisticians have developed methods to address these non-compliance and non-response problems. Much of this literature builds on the insights of the method of instrumental variables (IV). The standard IV model helps to address the problem of non-compliance, but it does not address the simultaneous problem of non-response. As a part of the research for this study, we developed a generalization of IV that addresses both non-compliance and non-response in a method called the Generalized Endogenous Treatment (GET) model. We use GET to identify the main causal effects we describe in this book. Here we first give the intuition behind the basic IV model's approach to non-compliance, and then we show how we extend IV to address the problem of non-response using GET.

While the underlying method of IV is technical, it is easy to understand the intuition for how it helps correct the noncompliance problem. In order to make use of IV, in addition to randomization, the exclusion restriction, and the absence of spillovers assumptions, we must assume that there are some participants who do comply with the protocol irrespective of whether they were assigned to the treatment or control groups. That is, we assume some "compliers" follow the solid lines of Figure A.1 irrespective of their assignment. There may very well be some "noncompliers" who follow the dotted paths and fail to comply with their assignments (who in the IV literature are labeled "never takers"), but the IV method makes use of the compliers to identify the causal effect.[2] The method only identifies the causal effect of the intervention on compliers, a quantity known as the complier average causal effect (CACE), rather than the causal effect on the full population of participants; this is a limitation in that the causal effect of the intervention might be very different

---

[2] Those familiar with the experimental noncompliance literature will also be familiar with a fifth assumption, called monotonicity, which generally requires that there are no participants who would do the opposite of their assignments in the experimental protocol. In our case, we do not need to evoke this assumption since participants cannot choose to participate in the DG condition if they are assigned to a control group, since we controlled admission to the events. Likewise, we do not need to consider the presence of "always takes" who always participate in the treatment even when assigned to control, for the same reason.

for compliers than noncompliers and we may be interested in the causal effect for everyone in the population.

To develop the quantity that estimates the causal effect of the intervention for compliers, first note that under randomization, the exclusion restriction assumption, and the assumption of no spillovers, the participants who are assigned to each experimental condition are comparable to each other. That is to say, as researchers we do not have control whether participants *comply* with their assignments, but we do have full control over which specific participants in our study were *assigned* to each condition, and so we can ensure that the participants *assigned* to each condition are similar to each other.

Now consider what happens to the group of participants assigned to the DG condition, and for purposes of illustration, assume the truth is that exposure to the intervention increased participants' policy knowledge. After we have assigned participants to DG, some will comply by reading the background materials and participating in the deliberative town hall, and so will experience the full effect of increased knowledge that comes from exposure to the intervention. Others however will not comply with these activities and so will not experience the effect of the intervention and so will not increase in their knowledge. In this illustration, the compliers assigned to DG will have higher scores on the policy quiz on the follow up survey, and the non-compliers will not. So the average of everyone assigned to the DG condition will show an increase in the knowledge scores, but a lower increase than the causal effect since the group mixes some compliers and non-compliers. This average of the scores among those assigned to the treatment, that ignores participants' actual exposure to the intervention, is called the "intention to treat" effect (ITT). The ITT is identifiable as a causal effect only under the three basic assumptions of randomization, no spillovers, and the exclusion restriction.

Under our simple illustration, the ITT is a combination of two quantities,

ITT = (percent of the DG that are compliers) × (causal effect on compliers) + (percent of DG that are non-compliers) × (causal effect on non-compliers)

Since the causal effect on non-compliers is equal to zero, the equation reduces to

ITT = (percent of the DG that are compliers) × (causal effect on compliers)

We have already shown that the ITT is identified in the data using only our three basic assumptions. To find the percent of the DG that are compliers, we simply divide the number of participants assigned to the DG condition who participated by the total number who were assigned to the DG condition, so that quantity is also identified in the data. So we can retrieve the causal effect on compliers, or the CACE, by rearranging the previous equation to yield:

CACE = ITT/(percent of the DG that are compliers)

which is also known as the IV estimand. Thus, using the method of IV, and for now ignoring the simultaneous problem of non-response, we can identify and estimate the causal effect of the intervention among the subgroup of participants who are compliers, even though we know there is a non-random subset of participants mixed in who are non-compliers.

In our research, we made extensive use of the IV method to identify the causal effect of exposure to the DG online deliberative town halls on the extent to which the House members persuaded participants on the merits of their positions on immigration policy, which we report in Chapter 5, as well as the effect of the sessions on trust in and approval of the representative, which we report on in Chapter 6. Finally, we use IV to study whether the results from the House experiments replicated in the larger sessions with Sen. Levin that focused on terrorist detainee policy. We report the results of this replication study in Chapter 7. All of these results using the method of IV are described in our article "Field Experiment Evidence of Substantive, Attributional, and Behavioral Persuasion by Members of Congress in Online Town Halls," which appeared in the *Proceedings of the National Academy of Sciences*, Volume 112, pages 3937–42. This PNAS paper was coauthored with our colleague William Minozzi, who is a professor of political science at The Ohio State University.

As we mention above, a main limitation of the IV method is that it cannot address the simultaneous problem of non-response on the follow up survey.[3] Another limitation is that it only identifies the causal effect of the intervention on the subset of compliers. Our experiment provided us

---

[3] To address this limitation in our PNAS paper, we made extensive use of robustness tests to demonstrate that in the specific case of our study, the pattern of missing data did not have an effect on the conclusions we drew from the IV analysis. In the typical case, however, this is unlikely to be true. In addition, we separately replicated these IV results in a separate analysis using the GET model that we describe next, a model that accounts for missing data.

with an opportunity to extend the method of IV by developing the GET model to address these two limitations. We describe the GET model in detail in the article "Estimating Treatment Effects in the Presence of Non-Compliance and Non-Response: The GET Model," which appeared in the journal *Political Analysis,* Volume 19, pages 205–26.

Like IV, the underlying methods of GET are very technical, but the intuition is easy to convey. The heart of GET is a novel method to measure each participant's unobserved propensity to comply with the study protocol, which combines our observations of the many opportunities the study participants have to participate or decline to participate in our study to estimate each participant's propensity to participate. And once we have an estimate of the compliance type the analysis is very straightforward in that we can compare outcomes among those at a given level of the compliance measure who participated in the deliberative town hall to those with a similar compliance score who did not participate; that is, comparing likely compliers who participated in the deliberative town hall to likely compliers who did not participate, and likely non-compliers who participated (perhaps despite their inclinations) to likely non-compliers who did not participate. In all cases, GET compares apples to apples and oranges to oranges to evaluate the effect of the intervention for all participants, even non-compliers, and so we can state such quantities as the CACE, the non-complier causal effect, and even the causal effect for the full set of participants.

The key to GET the model's ability to measure the propensity to comply with the study protocol for each participant, including those assigned to the control groups, while as we note above IV can only distinguish the compliers among those assigned to the active treatment. To see how this works for GET, Figure A.1 shows that we give each participant several opportunities to participate or decline to participate in the study protocol, depending on their assignment. Those assigned to the TC condition are given the opportunity to respond or not respond to the follow up survey and to the November survey. Those assigned to the IO condition are given these opportunities and in addition the opportunity to respond to the survey on the background materials. Finally, those assigned to the DG condition are given all of these opportunities plus the opportunity to participate in the session. Thus, by the completion of the study, the participants have generated a considerable amount of behavioral data on their compliance type, and the GET model uses those data and a measurement model to estimate the compliance type for each participant, irrespective of which condition they were assigned. Indeed, the very fact that many participants fail to comply with the study protocol is what enables GET to measure all participants' compliance type.

Having this measure of compliance type also allows us to address the simultaneous problem of survey non-response. Here we make one additional assumption, which is that the personality characteristics that lead participants not to comply with the intervention are the same characteristics that lead participants not to respond to the follow up survey. That is, we need to posit that there is one set of characteristics that leads participants to fail to comply with all aspects of the study protocol, whether that is participating in the DG or responding to the surveys, and that this propensity is measured in our compliance type variable. Under this assumption, the follow up survey responses are missing at random conditional on this variable. Given this additional assumption, holding constant compliance type, we can impute the missing follow up survey data based on the information we have about each participant in a manner that is unbiased and incorporates the remaining statistical uncertainty that we have in that imputation to yield correct statistical inferences.

We used GET to estimate the effect of exposure to the DG online deliberative town hall platform on the extent to which participants in the DG session gained policy knowledge relevant to immigration policy, which we report on in Chapter 4. The underlying results on which Chapter 4 relies were originally published in the article entitled "Means, Motive, and Opportunity in Becoming Informed about Politics: A Deliberative Field Experiments with Members of Congress and their Constituents," which was published in the journal *Public Opinion Quarterly*, Volume 75, pages 483–503. The replication results of these findings on policy knowledge in the larger Levin study that we report in Chapter 7 also make use of GET. Finally, the results that we report in Chapter 6 on the increase in DG participants' external (but not internal) self-efficacy also make use of the GET model and were originally published in the technical paper on GET that appeared in *Political Analysis* that we cite above.

References

Achen, Christopher H., and Larry M. Bartels. *Democracy for Realists: Why Elections Do Not Produce Responsive Government*. Princeton, NJ: Princeton University Press, 2016.

Adams, John. "John Adams to Mercy Otis Warren." National Archives. April 16, 1776. https://founders.archives.gov/documents/Adams/06-04-02-0044 *The Works of John Adams, Vol. 4: Novanglus, Thoughts on Government, Defence of the Constitution*. Altenmünster, Germany: Jazzybee Verlag, 2015.

Alsalam, Nabeel. "Role of Immigrants in the U.S. Labor Market: An Update." Washington, DC: Congressional Budget Office, 2010, Accessed May 28, 2018. www.cbo.gov/sites/default/files/cbofiles/ftpdocs/116xx/doc11691/07 -23-immigrants_in_labor_force.pdf.

Althaus, Scott L. *Collective Preferences in Democratic Politics: Opinion Surveys and the Will of the People*. Cambridge: Cambridge University Press, 2003.

Anderson, Ashley A., Dominique Brossard, Dietram A. Scheufele, Michael A. Xenos, and Peter Ladwig. "The 'nasty Effect': Online Incivility and Risk Perceptions of Emerging Technologies." *Journal of Computer-Mediated Communication: JCMC* 19, no. 3 (2014): 373–87.

Bächtiger, André, and Marina Lindell. "'Benchmarking' Deliberative Quality across Sites." *Political Communication* 26, Fall (2016): 1–2.

Bächtiger, André, and John Parkinson. *Mapping and Measuring Deliberation: Micro and Marco Knowledge of Deliberative Quality, Dynamics and Contexts*. Oxford: Oxford University Press, 2018.

Bächtiger, André, Simon Niemeyer, Michael Neblo, Marco R. Steenbergen, and Jürg Steiner. "Disentangling Diversity in Deliberative Democracy: Competing Theories, Their Blind Spots and Complementarities." *Journal of Political Philosophy* 18, no. 1 (2010): 32–63.

Bakshy, Eytan, Solomon Messing, and Lada A. Adamic. "Exposure to Ideologically Diverse News and Opinion on Facebook." *Science* 348, no. 6239 (June 5, 2015): 1130–2.

Bartels, Larry M. *Unequal Democracy: The Political Economy of the New Gilded Age.* Princeton, NJ: Princeton University Press, 2009.

Berinsky, Adam J. "Rumors and Health Care Reform: Experiments in Political Misinformation." *British Journal of Political Science* 47, no. 2 (2017): 241–62.

Bianco, William T. *Trust: Representatives and Constituents.* Ann Arbor: University of Michigan Press, 1994.

Bishop, Bill. *The Big Sort: Why the Clustering of Like-Minded America Is Tearing Us Apart.* New York, NY: Houghton Mifflin Harcourt, 2009.

Blake, Aaron. "President Obama's Farewell Speech Transcript, Annotated." *Washington Post.* January 10, 2017. www.washingtonpost.com/news/the-fix/wp/2017/01/10/president-obamas-farewell-speech-transcript-annotated/

Boeckmann, Robert J., and Tom R. Tyler. "Trust, Respect, and the Psychology of Political Engagement." *Journal of Applied Social Psychology* 32, no. 10 (2002): 2067–88.

Burden, Collin, Tim Hysom, Kevin M. Esterling, David Lazer, and Michael Neblo. "*2007 Gold Mouse Report: Lessons from the Best Web Sites on Capitol Hill.*" Washington, DC: Congressional Management Foundation, 2007.

Cacioppo, John T., Richard E. Petty, and Chuan Feng Kao. "The Efficient Assessment of Need for Cognition." *Journal of Personality Assessment* 48, no. 3 (1984): 306–7.

Cain, Bruce E. *Democracy More or Less: America's Political Reform Quandary.* Cambridge: Cambridge University Press, 2014.

Canes-Wrone, Brandice. *Who Leads Whom?: Presidents, Policy, and the Public.* Chicago, IL: University of Chicago Press, 2010.

Carpenter, Daniel P., Kevin M. Esterling, and David M. J. Lazer. "Friends, Brokers, and Transitivity: Who Informs Whom in Washington Politics?" *Journal of Politics* 66, no. 1 (2004): 224–46.

Centola, Damon, and Michael Macy. "Complex Contagions and the Weakness of Long Ties." *American Journal of Sociology* 113, no. 3 (2007): 702–34.

Chadwick, Andrew. "Web 2.0: New Challenges for the Study of E-Democracy in an Era of Informational Exuberance." *I/S: A Journal of Law and Policy for the Information Society* 5 (2008): 9–10.

Cheatham, Lauren B., and Zakary L. Tormala. "The Curvilinear Relationship between Attitude Certainty and Attitudinal Advocacy." *Personality and Social Psychology Bulletin* 43, no. 1 (2017): 3–16.

Chen, Gina Masullo. *Online Incivility and Public Debate: Nasty Talk.* New York: Palgrave Macmillan, 2017.

Chong, Dennis, and James N. Druckman. "Framing Public Opinion in Competitive Democracies." *The American Political Science Review* 101, no. 4 (November 2007): 637–55.

Cohen, Joshua. "Deliberation and Democratic Legitimacy." In *The Good Polity*, edited by Alan Hamlin, and Philip Pettit, 17–34. New York, NY: Basil Blackwell, 1989.

Coleman, Stephen, and Peter M. Shane. *Connecting Democracy: Online Consultation and the Flow of Political Communication.* Cambridge, MA: MIT Press, 2011.

Cook, Fay Lomax, Michael X. Delli Carpini, and Lawrence R. Jacobs "Who Deliberates? Discursive Participation in America." In *Deliberation,*

Participation and Democracy: Can the People Govern?, edited by Shawn W. Rosenberg, 25–44. London: Palgrave Macmillan, 2007.

Dahl, Robert A. *Democracy and Its Critics*. New Haven, CT: Yale University Press, 1992.

DeBonis, Mike. "Rep. Charlie Dent, Outspoken GOP Moderate, Will Not Seek Reelection." *Washington Post*. September 07, 2017. www.washingtonpost .com/news/powerpost/wp/2017/09/07/rep-charlie-dent-outspoken-gop-moderate-will-not-seek-reelection/?tid=a_inl&utm_term=.a1fbba322114

Delli Carpini, Michael X., and Scott Keeter. "Measuring Political Knowledge: Putting First Things First." *American Journal of Political Science* 37, no. 4 (November 1993): 1179–206.

What Americans Know about Politics and Why It Matters. New Haven, CT: Yale University Press, 1996.

DePaulo, Bella M., James J. Lindsay, Brian E. Malone, et al. "Cues to Deception." *Psychological Bulletin* 129, no. 1 (January 2003): 74–118.

Dewey, John. *The Public and Its Problems*. Athens, OH: Swallow Press, 1954.

Diwakar, Rekha. "Local Contest, National Impact: Understanding the Success of India's Aam Aadmi Party in the 2015 Delhi Assembly Election." *Representation* 52, no. 1 (2016): 71–80.

Douglas Arnold, R. *The Logic of Congressional Action*. New Haven, CT: Yale University Press, 1992.

Druckman, James N., Matthew S. Levendusky, and Audrey McLain. "No Need to Watch: How the Effects of Partisan Media Can Spread via Interpersonal Discussions." *American Journal of Political Science* 62, no. 1 (2017): 99–112.

Eliasoph, Nina. *Avoiding Politics: How Americans Produce Apathy in Everyday Life*. Cambridge: Cambridge University Press, 1998.

Elizabeth, Mendes. "*Americans Down on Congress, OK with Own Representative*." Washington, DC: Gallup. May 9, 2013. www.gallup.com/poll/162362/americans-down-congress-own-representative.aspx

Elliot, Jonathan. *The Debates in the Several State Conventions on the Adoption of the Federal Constitution: As Recommended by the General Convention at Philadelphia in 1787*. Vol. 2, 1866 (reprinted 1937). Published under the Sanction of Congress, Accessed May 28, 2018. https://memory.loc.gov/cgi-bin/query/r?ammem/hlaw:@field(DOCID+@lit(ed0021)).

Elseay, Jennifer K. *Treatment of Battlefield Detainees in the War on Terrorism*. Order Code RL31367. Congressional Research Service, updated 2007. https://fas.org/sgp/crs/terror/RL31367.pdf

Erikson, Robert S., Michael B. MacKuen, and James A. Stimson. *The Macro Polity*. Cambridge: Cambridge University Press, 2002.

Esterling, Kevin M. "Public Outreach: The Cornerstone of Judicial Independence." *Judicature* 82, no. 3 (1998): 112.

The Political Economy of Expertise: Information and Efficiency in American National Politics. Ann Arbor: University of Michigan Press, 2004.

Esterling, Kevin M., David M. J. Lazer, and Michael A. Neblo. "Improving Congressional Websites." Center for Technology Innovation at Brookings, 2010.

"Representative Communication: Web Site Interactivity and Distributional Path Dependence in the U.S. Congress." *Political Communication* 28, no. 4 (2011): 409–39.

"Connecting to Constituents." *Political Research Quarterly* 66, no. 1 (2012): 102–14.

Esterling, Kevin M., Michael A. Neblo, and David M. J. Lazer. "Estimating Treatment Effects in the Presence of Noncompliance and Nonresponse: The Generalized Endogenous Treatment Model." *Political Analysis* 19, no. 2 (Spring 2011): 205–26.

"Means, Motive, and Opportunity in Becoming Informed about Politics: A Deliberative Field Experiment Involving Members of Congress and Their Constituents." *Public Opinion Quarterly* 75, no. 3 (Fall 2011): 483–503.

Esterling, Kevin M., Michael A. Neblo, David M. J. Lazer, and William Minozzi. "The Role of Familiarity in Democratic Representation: A Field Experiment on Constituent Attitudes toward Members of Congress." Paper presented at the 2015 meeting of the American Political Science Association.

Etzioni, Amitai. "Minerva: An Electronic Town Hall." *Policy Sciences* 3, no. 4 (1972): 457–74.

Etzioni, Amitai, Kenneth Laudon, and Sara Lipson. "Participatory Technology: The MINERVA Communications Tree." *Journal of Communication* 25, no. 2 (June 1, 1975): 64–74.

Fenno, Richard F. *Home Style: House Members in Their Districts*. Boston, MA: Little, Brown and Co., 1978.

The Challenge of Congressional Representation. Cambridge, MA: Harvard University Press, 2013.

Finkel, Steven E. "Reexamining the 'Minimal Effects' Model in Recent Presidential Campaigns." *Journal of Politics* 55, no. 1 (1993): 1–21.

Fiorina, Morris P., and David W. Rohde, eds. *Home Style and Washington Work: Studies of Congressional Politics*. Ann Arbor: University of Michigan Press, 1991.

Fishkin, James S. *Democracy and Deliberation: New Directions for Democratic Reform*. New Haven, CT: Yale University Press, 1991.

Fishkin, James S., Robert C. Luskin, and Alice Siu. "Europolis and the European Public Sphere: Empirical Explorations of a Counterfactual Ideal." *European Union Politics* 15, no. 3 (May 16, 2014): 328–51.

Flynn, D. J., Brendan Nyhan, and Jason Reifler. "The Nature and Origins of Misperceptions: Understanding False and Unsupported Beliefs about Politics." *Political Psychology* 38, no. S1 (February 1, 2017): 127–50.

Fountain, Jane E. *Building the Virtual State: Information Technology and Institutional Change*. Washington, DC: Brookings Institution Press, 2001.

Fox, Justin, and Kenneth W. Shotts. "Delegates or Trustees? A Theory of Political Accountability." *The Journal of Politics* 71, no. 4 (2009): 1225–37.

Gallup, "Congress and the Public." Washington DC: Gallup. Accessed May 28, 2018. www.gallup.com/poll/1600/congress-public.aspx

Garfinkle, Adam. *Broken: American Political Dysfunction and What to Do about It*. Washington, DC: American Interest EBooks, 2013.

Gastil, John, Chiara Bacci, and Michael Dollinger. "Is Deliberation Neutral? Patterns of Attitude Change during 'The Deliberative Polls™'," *Journal of Public Deliberation* 6, no. 2 (2010), Article 3.

Gerber, Marlène, André Bächtiger, Irena Fiket, Marco Steenbergen, and Jürg Steiner. "Deliberative and Non-Deliberative Persuasion: Mechanisms of Opinion Formation in EuroPolis." *European Union Politics* 15, no. 3 (2014): 410–29.

Gerber, Marlène, André Bächtiger, Susumu Shikano, Simon Reber, and Samuel Rohr. "Deliberative Abilities and Influence in a Transnational Deliberative Poll (EuroPolis)." *British Journal of Political Science* (2016), Accessed May 28, 2018. www.cambridge.org/core/journals/british-journal-of-political-science/article/deliberativeabilities-and-influence-in-a-transnational-deliberative-poll-europolis/F8488E7C93866843A2D23520572C665A.

Gerber, Elisabeth R., Arthur Lupia, Mathew D. McCubbins, and D. Roderick Kiewiet. *Stealing the Initiative: How State Government Responds to Direct Democracy. Real Politics in America.* Upper Saddle River, NJ: Prentice Hall, 2001.

Goold, Susan Dorr, Michael A. Neblo, Scott Y. H. Kim, et al. "What Is Good Public Deliberation?" *The Hastings Center Report* 42, no. 2 (2012): 24–6.

Gottfried, Jeffrey, and Elisa Shearer. "News Use across Social Media Platforms 2016." Washington, DC: Pew Research Center, 2016.

Granovetter, Mark S. "Strength of Weak Ties." *American Journal of Sociology* 78, no. 6 (1973): 1360–80.

Gutmann, Amy, and Dennis Thompson. *Why Deliberative Democracy?* Princeton, NJ: Princeton University Press, 2004.

Habermas, Jürgen. *Between Facts and Norms: Contributions to a Discourse Theory of Law and Democracy.* William Rehg, Translator. Cambridge, MA: MIT Press, 1996.

Hacker, Jacob S., and Paul Pierson. *Off Center: The Republican Revolution and the Erosion of American Democracy.* New Haven, CT: Yale University Press, 2006.

Hampton, Keith N., Lee Rainie, Weixu Lu, et al. "*Social Media and the 'Spiral of Silence'.*" Washington, DC: Pew Research Internet Project, 2014.

Heclo, Hugh. "Issue Networks and the Executive Establishment." In *The New American Political System*, edited by Anthony King, 87–124. Washington, DC: American Enterprise Institute, 1978.

Hibbing, John R., and Elizabeth Theiss-Morse. *Congress as Public Enemy: Public Attitudes toward American Political Institutions.* Cambridge: Cambridge University Press, 1995.

Stealth Democracy: Americans' Beliefs about How Government Should Work. Cambridge: Cambridge University Press, 2002.

Holland, Paul W. "Statistics and Causal Inference." *Journal of the American Statistical Association* 81, no. 396 (1986): 945–60.

Jacobs, Lawrence R., Fay Lomax Cook, and Michael X. Delli Carpini. *Talking Together: Public Deliberation and Political Participation in America.* Chicago, IL: University of Chicago Press, 2009.

Jacobs, Lawrence R., and Robert Y. Shapiro. *Politicians Don't Pander: Political Manipulation and the Loss of Democratic Responsiveness.* Chicago, IL: University of Chicago Press, 2000.

Jarvis, W. Blair G., and Richard E. Petty. "The Need to Evaluate." *Journal of Personality and Social Psychology* 70, no. 1 (1996): 172.

James, Madison. *"The Federalist #55."* New York Packet, Accessed May 28, 2018. www.congress.gov/resources/display/content/The+Federalist+Papers #TheFederalistPapers-55

Karpowitz, Christopher F., and Chad Raphael. *Deliberation, Democracy, and Civic Forums: Improving Equality and Publicity.* Cambridge: Cambridge University Press, 2014.

Kathy, Goldschmidt, Nicole Folk, Cooper, and Bradford, Fitch. "Communicating with Congress: How Citizen Advocacy Is Changing Mail Operations on Capitol Hill." Washington, DC: Congressional Management Foundation, 2011, Accessed May 28, 2018. www.congressfoundation.org/storage/documents/CMF_Pubs/cwc-mail-operations.pdf.

Katz, Elihu, and Paul Felix Lazarsfeld. *Personal Influence: The Part Played by People in the Flow of Mass Communications.* New York, NY: Free Press, 1955.

Kennedy, Ryan, Anand Sokhey, David Lazer, Michael Neblo, and Kevin Esterling. "Gender, Deliberation and (Equal?) Voice: Evidence from Online Town Halls." Paper presented at the 2015 meeting of the Midwest Political Science Association.

Kinder, Donald R. "Communication and Politics in the Age of Information." In *Oxford Handbook of Political Psychology*, edited by D. O. Sears, L. Huddy, and R. Jervis, 357–93. New York, NY: Oxford University Press, 2003.

King, Gary, Jennifer Pan, and Margaret E. Roberts. "How the Chinese Government Fabricates Social Media Posts for Strategic Distraction, Not Engaged Argument." *American Political Science Review* 111, no. 3 (August 2017): 484–501.

Kingdon, John W. *Congressmen's Voting Decisions.* Ann Arbor: University of Michigan Press, 1989.

Klein, Ezra. "The Single Most Important Fact about American Politics." *Vox.* June 13, 2014. www.vox.com/2014/6/13/5803768/pew-most-important-fact-american-politics

Lafont, Cristina. "Can Democracy Be Deliberative & Participatory? The Democratic Case for Political Uses of Mini-Publics." *Daedalus* 146, no. 3 (2017): 85–105.

Lazer, David, Ines Mergel, Curtis Ziniel, Kevin M. Esterling, and Michael A. Neblo. "The Multiple Institutional Logics of Innovation." *International Public Management Journal* 14, no. 3 (2011): 311–40.

Lazer, David, M. Neblo, K. Esterling, and K. Goldschmidt. *"Online Town Hall Meetings: Exploring Democracy in the 21st Century."* Washington, DC: Congressional Management Foundation, 2009.

Lazer, David, Michael Neblo, and Kevin Esterling. "The Internet and the Madisonian Cycle: Possibilities and Prospects for Consultative Representation." In *Connecting Democracy: Online Consultation and the Flow of Political Communication*, edited by Stephen Coleman, and Peter Shane, 265–85. Cambridge, MA: MIT Press, 2011.

Lazer, David M., Anand E. Sokhey, Michael A. Neblo, Kevin M. Esterling, and Ryan Kennedy. "Expanding the Conversation: Multiplier Effects from a Deliberative Field Experiment." *Political Communication* 32, no. 4 (2015): 552–73.

Lessig, Lawrence. *Republic Lost: How Money Corrupts Congress – And a Plan to Stop It*. New York, NY: Twelve, 2011.

Levine, Michael E., and Jennifer L. Forrence. "Regulatory Capture, Public Interest, and the Public Agenda: Toward a Synthesis." *Journal of Law, Economics, & Organization* 6 (1990): 167–98.

Lindell, Marina, André Bächtiger, Kimmo Grönlund, et al. "What Drives the Polarisation and Moderation of Opinions? Evidence from a Finnish Citizen Deliberation Experiment on Immigration." *European Journal of Political Research* 56, no. 1 (2017): 23–45.

Lodge, Milton, Kathleen M. McGraw, and Partick Stroh. "An Impression-Driven Model of Candidate Evaluation." *The American Political Science Review* 83, no. 2 (June 1989): 399–419.

Lupia, Arthur, and James N. Druckman. "Preference Change in Competitive Political Environments." *Annual Review of Political Science* 19, no. 1 (2016): 13–31.

Mann, Thomas E., and Norman J. Ornstein. *It's Even Worse Than It Looks: How the American Constitutional System Collided with the New Politics of Extremism*. New York, NY: Basic Books, 2016.

Mansbridge, Jane. *Beyond Adversary Democracy*. Chicago, IL: University of Chicago Press, 1983.

"Everyday Talk in the Deliberative System." In *Deliberative Politics: Essays on Democracy and Disagreement*, edited by Stephen Macedo, 1–211. Oxford: Oxford University Press, 1999.

"Clarifying the Concept of Representation." *The American Political Science Review* 105, no. 3 (August 2011): 621–30.

"A Contingency Theory of Accountability." In *The Oxford Handbook of Public Accountability* edited by Mark Bovens, Robert E. Goodin, and Thomas Schillemans, 55–68. Oxford, UK: Oxford University Press 2014.

Marcus, George E., W. Russell Neuman, and Michael MacKuen. *Affective Intelligence and Political Judgment*. Chicago, IL: University of Chicago Press, 2000.

Mendelberg, Tali, and John Oleske. "Race and Public Deliberation." *Political Communication* 17, no. 2 (2000): 169–91.

Minozzi, William, Michael A. Neblo, Kevin M. Esterling, and David M. J. Lazer. "Field Experiment Evidence of Substantive, Attributional, and Behavioral Persuasion by Members of Congress in Online Town Halls." *Proceedings of the National Academy of Sciences*, 2015.

Murphy, DeAmo. *The Michigan Chronicle*, 2007.

Mutz, Diana C. "Cross-Cutting Social Networks: Testing Democratic Theory in Practice." *American Political Science Review* 96, no. 1 (2002): 111–26.

Hearing the Other Side: Deliberative versus Participatory Democracy. Cambridge: Cambridge University Press, 2006.

NCOA "9 Tips for Town Hall Meetings." NCOA. August 11, 2017. www .ncoa.org/public-policy-action/advocacy-toolkit/meeting-with-congress/ town-hall-tips/

Neblo, Michael A. "Giving Hands and Feet to Morality." *Perspectives on Politics* 2, no. 1 (2004): 99–100.

"Thinking through Democracy: Between the Theory and Practice of Deliberative Politics." *Acta Politica* 40, no. 2 (2005): 169–81.

"Family Disputes: Diversity in Defining and Measuring Deliberation." *Swiss Political Science Review* 13, no. 4 (December 1, 2007): 527–57.

"Philosophical Psychology with Political Intent." In *The Affect Effect*, edited by W. Russell Neuman, George E. Marcus, Michael MacKuen, and Ann N. Crigler, 25–47. Chicago, IL: University of Chicago Press, 2007.

"Deliberation's Legitimation Crisis." *Critical Review* 23, no. 3 (2011): 405–19.

"Reform Pluralism as Political Theology and Democratic Technology." *Election Law Journal* 13, no. 4 (2014): 526–33.

Deliberative Democracy between Theory and Practice. Cambridge: Cambridge University Press, 2015.

Neblo, Michael A., Daniel O. Davis, Robert Gulotty, Christina V. Xydias, and Daniel J. Blake. "Measuring Sincerity and the Substantive Content of Arguments in Deliberation." Program on Networked Governance Working Paper PNG No.PNG08–001.

Neblo, Michael A., Kevin M. Esterling, Ryan P. Kennedy, David M. J. Lazer, and Anand E. Sokhey. "Who Wants to Deliberate – And Why?" *The American Political Science Review* 104, no. 3 (August 2010): 566–83.

Neblo, Michael A., William Minozzi, Kevin M. Esterling, et al. "The Need for a Translational Science of Democracy." *Science* 355, no. 6328 (March 3, 2017): 914–15.

Norris, Pippa. *Democratic Deficit: Critical Citizens Revisited*. Cambridge: Cambridge University Press, 2011.

Noveck, Beth Simone. *Smart Citizens, Smarter State: The Technologies of Expertise and the Future of Governing*. Cambridge, MA: Harvard University Press, 2015.

Page, Benjamin I., and Robert Y. Shapiro. *The Rational Public: Fifty Years of Trends in Americans' Policy Preferences*. Chicago, IL: University of Chicago Press, 2010.

Pariser, Eli. *The Filter Bubble: How the New Personalized Web Is Changing What We Read and How We Think*. London: Penguin, 2011.

"Paul Lazarsfeld." Wikiquote, Accessed May 28, 2018. https://en.wikiquote .org/wiki/Paul_Lazarsfeld

Pitkin, Hanna Fenichel. *The Concept of Representation*. Berkeley: University of California Press, 1967.

"Representation and Democracy: Uneasy Alliance." *Scandinavian Political Studies* 27, no. 3 (September 1, 2004): 335–42.

Posner, Richard A. *Law, Pragmatism, and Democracy*. Cambridge, MA: Harvard University Press, 2005.

Pritts, Joy L., Michael A. Neblo, Laura J. Damschroder, and Rodney A. Hayward. "Veterans' Views on Balancing Privacy and Research in Medicine: A Deliberative Democratic Study." *Michigan State University Journal of Medicine and Law* 12 (2008): 17.

Przybyla, Heidi M. "Republicans Avoid Town Halls after Health Care Votes." *USA Today*. April 11, 2017. www.usatoday.com/story/news/politics/2017/04/10/ republicans-avoid-town-halls-after-health-care-votes/100286290/

Rauch, Jonathan. "How American Politics Went Insane." *Atlantic.* July 2016. http://people.ucls.uchicago.edu/~cjuriss/US/Documents/US-Jurisson-How-American-Politics-Became-So-Ineffective-Atlantic-2016-07.pdf

Rheingold, Howard. *The Virtual Community: Finding Connection in a Computerized World.* Boston, MA: Addison-Wesley Longman Publishing Co., Inc., 1993.

Rosenblum, Nancy L. *On the Side of the Angels: An Appreciation of Parties and Partisanship.* Princeton, NJ: Princeton University Press, 2008.

Rubin, Donald. "Estimating Causal Effects of Treatments in Randomized and Nonrandomized Studies," *Journal of Educational Psychology* 66, no. 5 (1974) 688–701.

Sanders, Lynn M. "Against Deliberation." *Political Theory* 25, no. 3 (1997): 347–76.

Selena, Caldera, and Paige Piper/Bach. "Immigration Policy in the United States." Congressional Budget Office, February 2006. Accessed May 28, 2018. www.cbo.gov/publication/17625

Skocpol, Theda. *Diminished Democracy: From Membership to Management in American Civic Life.* Norman, OK: University of Oklahoma Press, 2013.

Smith, Samantha. "A Wider Ideological Gap between More and Less Educated Adults." *Pew Research Center for the People and the Press.* April 26, 2016. www.people-press.org/2016/04/26/a-wider-ideological-gap-between-more-and-less-educated-adults/

Snyder, Timothy. *On Tyranny: Twenty Lessons from the Twentieth Century.* New York, NY: Tim Duggan Books, 2017.

Sparrow, Betsy, Jenny Liu, and Daniel M. Wegner. "Google Effects on Memory: Cognitive Consequences of Having Information at Our Fingertips." *Science* 333, no. (6043)(August 5, 2011): 776–78.

Stasser, Garold, and William Titus. "Hidden Profiles: A Brief History." *Psychological Inquiry* 14, no. 3–4 (2003): 304–13.

Steiner, Jürg, Andrè Bächtiger, Markus Spörndli, and Marco R. Steenbergen. *Deliberative Politics in Action: Analysing Parliamentary Discourse.* New York, NY: Cambridge University Press, 2004.

Steinhauer, Jennifer, and David M. Herszenhorn. "Congress Recesses, Leaving More Stalemates Than Accomplishments." *New York Times.* July 14, 2016. www.nytimes.com/2016/07/15/us/politics/congress-recesses-leaving-more-stalemates-than-accomplishments.html

Suiter, Jane, David Farrell, and Clodagh Harris. "The Irish Constitutional Convention: A Case of 'High Legitimacy'?" In *Constitutional Deliberative Democracy in Europe*, edited by Min Reuchamps, and Jane Suiter, 33–52. London, UK: ECPR Press, 2016.

Sunstein, Cass R. *Republic.com 2.0.* Princeton, NJ: Princeton University Press, 2008.

    #Republic: Divided Democracy in the Age of Social Media. Princeton, NJ: Princeton University Press, 2017.

Tani, Maxwell. "John Boehner Just Gave an Emotional Last Speech." *Business Insider.* October 29, 2015. www.businessinsider.com/john-boehner-last-speech-2015-10

Tetlock, Phillip. E., Linda Skitka, and Richard Boettger. "Social and Cognitive Strategies for Coping with Accountability: Conformity, Complexity, and Bolstering."*Journal of Personality and Social Psychology* 57, no. 4 (October 1989): 632–40.

Tufekci, Zeynep. *Twitter and Tear Gas: The Power and Fragility of Networked Protest*. New Haven, CT: Yale University Press, 2017.

Twain, Mark, and John S. Tuckey. *Mark Twain's Fables of Man*. Berkeley: University of California Press, 1972.

The AP-NORC Center for Public Affairs Research, Chicago, US. *"Views on Power and Influence in Washington."* APNORC.org. www.apnorc.org/projects/Pages/Power-and-Influence-in-Washington.aspx

Volden, Craig, and Alan E. Wiseman. *Legislative Effectiveness in the United States Congress: The Lawmakers*. New York, NY: Cambridge University Press, 2014.

"Voteview.com." Voteview. Accessed May 28, 2018. https://voteview.com

Weisman, Jonathan, and Shallagh Murray. "GOP Plans Hearings on Issue of Immigrants." *Washington Post*. June 21, 2006. www.washingtonpost.com/wp-dyn/content/article/2006/06/20/AR2006062000926.html

Wright, Scott. "Politics as Usual? Revolution, Normalization and a New Agenda for Online Deliberation." *New Media & Society* 14, no. 2 (August 5, 2011): 244–61.

Zeleny, Jeff. "Democrats Skip Town Halls to Avoid Voter Rage." *New York Times*. June 6, 2010. www.nytimes.com/2010/06/07/us/politics/07townhall.html

Index

Books in the series